Disaster Zone
Christoph Draeger

Lakehurst, New Jersey
Zeppelin Museum Friedrichshafen
Friedrichshafen, Germany
Sep 23 – Nov 7 1999

Action//Time//Vision (Alternative TV)
Orchard Gallery
Derry, Northern Ireland
June 26 – July 31 1999

Serneus New York retour
Kulturhaus Rosengarten
Grüsch, Switzerland
Oct 3 – Nov 15 1998

and in collaboration with
Galerie Urs Meile,
Lucerne, Switzerland

Lakehurst, N.J.
Zeppelin Museum Friedrichshafen, 1999

Lakehurst, New Jersey, Aug 13 1999
#37 from the series *Voyages apocalyptiques*,
C-Print, 46 x 58 cm

Crash, video stills
Video, 10 min, 1999
(from *The Hindenburg*)

Crash
Installation views *Lakehurst, N.J.*,
Zeppelin Museum Friedrichshafen,
1999
6 m³ puzzles, 2 video projectors,
4 speakers

Crash statistics, video still
Loop, 1999

Crash, video stills
Video, 10 min, 1999
(from *Airforce One, Fearless*)

Museé de l'air
Acrylic paint jet on pvc, 200 x 300 cm
Brussels, 1994

Crash, video stills
Video, 10 min, 1999
(from *Die hard 2, Kamikaze, Escape!,
The Hindenburg, Fearless*)

Earthquake revisited
Cinéma, Cinéma, Van Abbe Museum
Eindhoven, 1999
Ambisonic 4-channel sound installation
4-track minidisc player, 4 "Earthquake" Magma
15' inch sub woofers, 8 "Earthquake" full range
car speakers, garden house 4 x 4 x 4 m
In collaboration with Johannes Schütt
(Stills from *Earthquake*)

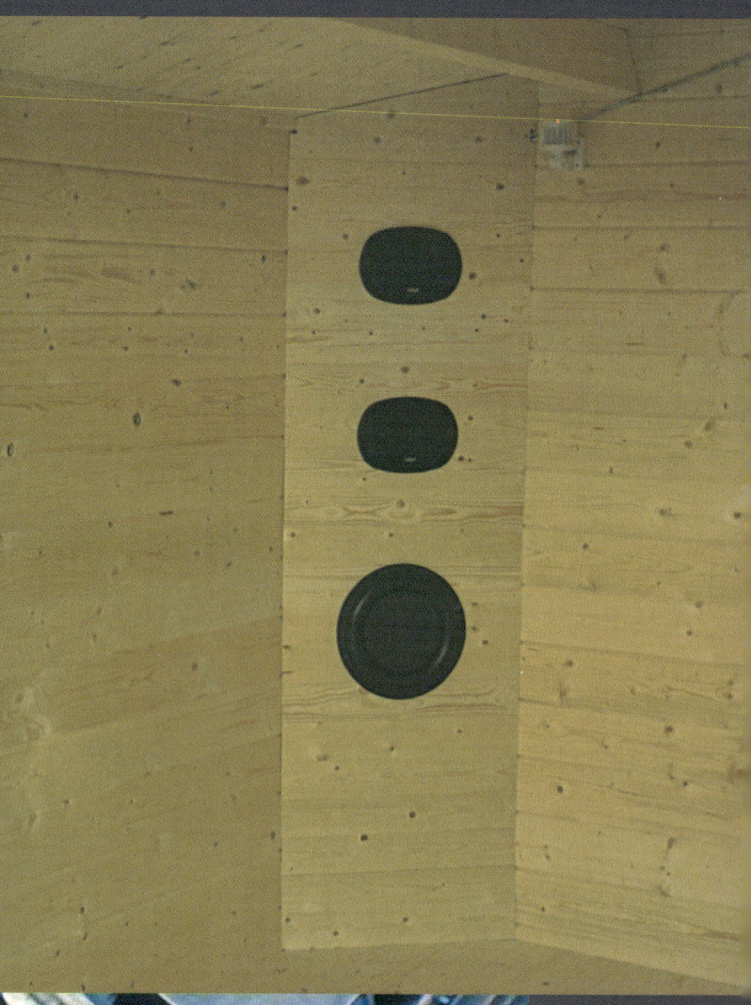

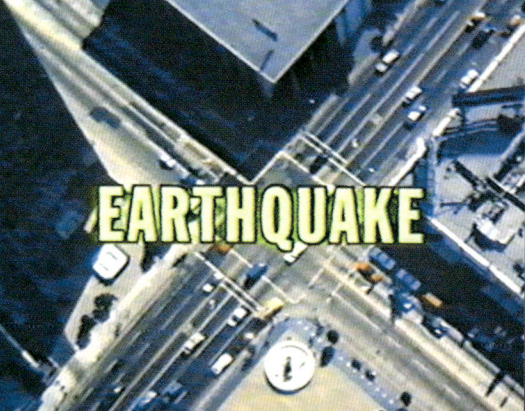

Hindenburg revisited
Lakehurst, NJ, Zeppelin Museum Friedrichshafen, 1999
Ambisonic 8-channel sound installation
(in the partial reconstruction of the airship Hindenburg)
8-track minidisc player, 16 loudspeakers
In collaboration with Johannes Schütt

Die Sicherheit des Risikos
Dirk Blübaum

Am 14. April 1912 sank der als unsinkbar geltende Luxusliner und das größte Schiff seiner Zeit, die Titanic, auf seiner Jungfernfahrt im Nordatlantik. Das Wunderwerk der Technik riß bei dieser wohl «schönsten» Katastrophe des 20. Jahrhunderts 1503 Menschen in den Tod. 15 Jahre später, am 6. Mai 1937, waren es 36 Menschen, die bei der noch heute berühmtesten Katastrophe der Luftfahrt, dem Hindenburg-Unglück in Lakehurst, ums Leben kamen. 1986 erlebte dann die westliche Raumfahrt ihren «schwarzen Freitag», als am 28. Januar die Raumfähre Challenger kurz nach dem Abheben von der Startrampe in 16 Kilometern Höhe explodierte. Alle sieben Astronauten fanden im Feuerball über Cape Canaveral den Tod.

In der Ausstellung *Lakehurst, New Jersey* im Zeppelin Museum Friedrichshafen bezieht sich Christoph Draeger nicht nur in besonderer Weise auf diesen Ort, sondern benutzt dessen Kontext, um uns den Spiegel unserer Technikgläubigkeit vorzuhalten. Puzzleteile und Katastrophenbilder werden in diesem Umfeld als Symbole lesbar, so daß die vermeintlichen Gegensätze zwischen diesen beiden Polen in konkreter Weise auf den konzeptuellen Ansatz zu verweisen vermögen. Während der Puzzlespieler sich nur deshalb auf sein Spiel so selbstvergessen zu konzentrieren vermag, weil die Welt um ihn herum «in Ordnung» ist, bezeichnet das Desaster genau den Zeitpunkt, in dem wir den sicheren Zugriff auf unsere Umwelt und unser Leben verlieren.

In seiner Installation stellt Draeger zwei Videos einander gegenüber: *Statistics* zeigt den fast meditativ beruhigenden und Sicherheit vermittelnden Blick aus dem Flugzeugfenster, während *Crash* eine Geschichte der Luftfahrt anhand ihrer Katastrophen nachzeichnet. Beginnend mit der Hindenburg-Katastrophe und dokumentarischen Aufnahmen aus dem Ersten und Zweiten Weltkrieg, zeigt das Video weiter in schneller Schnittfolge Sequenzen von Test-Crashs aus den 60er Jahren, um letztendlich in der reinen Hollywood-Fiktion der unzähligen *aircrash-movies* zu enden. In der Abfolge der Dokumentation von Realität über deren Manipulation bis hin zu ihrer Auflösung in der reinen Fiktion dechiffriert Draeger die Struktur unserer Realitätskonstruktion: Der Fiktion der Hollywood-Industrie wird unterbewußt die höchste Authentizität zuerkannt. Es sind diese Bilder, die auftauchen, wenn wir die Daten der 100 größten Flugkatastrophen dieses Jahrhunderts lesen, die in der Art eines Filmabspanns von unten nach oben vor dem Flugzeugfenster vorbeiziehen. So läßt uns Draeger jenes «aber es könnte doch» spüren, das jeder Flugpassagier beim Blick aus dem Fenster in den strahlend blauen Himmel so gern vergißt. Gleichzeitig untergräbt Draeger damit auch die grundsätzlich positive Darstellung der Technik im Zeppelin Museum: Dem Mythos

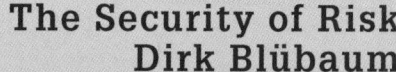

The Security of Risk
Dirk Blübaum

On April 14, 1912, the allegedly unsinkable luxury liner and largest ship of its time, the Titanic, sank into the North Atlantic on its maiden voyage. The wonders of the ship's technology brought 1503 people to their deaths in this catastrophe – probably the 20th century's most beautiful. Fifteen years later, on May 6, 1937, 36 people lost their lives in Lakehurst, New Jersey, in the Hindenburg disaster – to this day, most likely history's most famous air catastrophe. And on January 28, 1986, space travel experienced its "Black Friday" when the Space Shuttle Challenger exploded shortly after its launch only 16 kilometers into its journey. All seven astronauts perished in a ball of flames above Cape Canaveral.

In his exhibit *Lakehurst, New Jersey* at the Zeppelin Museum Friedrichshafen, Christoph Draeger is not only especially con-

des «Erhaben durch die Lüfte schweben» wird in erbarmungsloser Schärfe die Frage nach den Folgen des Versagens von Technik gegenübergestellt.

Diese Fragestellung wird noch erweitert, indem der Fußboden des Ausstellungsraumes mit fast zwei Tonnen Puzzleteilen bedeckt wurde. Die Unmenge von Bildfragmenten steht im Kontext der Medialisierung der Realität für jenen schier unermeßlichen Bildspeicher, aus dem die immer ähnlicher werdenden Bilder zusammengesetzt werden können. Auf haptischer Ebene gelingt es Draeger so, die grundsätzliche Dekonstruierbarkeit unserer Realitätsvorstellungen «ins Bild zu setzen», die ihre Basis in einer der Technikgläubigkeit analogen Bildergläubigkeit hat. Im Kontext dieser Realitätsdefiniton mußte in immer stärkerem Maße auf die Medialität und, aufgrund der zunehmenden Informationsdichte, auf die Kürze der Informationen geachtet werden. Unser Bild der Welt begann sich aus immer kleineren Informationsbausteinen zusammenzusetzen, die aber, in der Logik der Nachrichtensendungen, als ein einziges, geschlossenes Bild konsumiert werden sollten: das Welt-Bild als Puzzle.

Mit der Macht der Bilder wuchs auch die Beschränkung der Information auf jene Nachrichten, die nicht nur das Informationsbedürfnis einer möglichst großen Masse befriedigen, sondern zugleich große Aufmerksamkeit erregen konnten. Beides wird in hohem Maße von Katastrophen-Meldungen erfüllt. Nachrichten dieser Art spielen dabei gleich auf zweifache Weise mit unserem Begriff von wie auch unserer Suche nach Sicherheit: Zum einen wird die Katastrophe zum ästhetischen Spektakel, ohne

cerned with the exhibition venue, but also takes full advantage of its context, in order to reflect our belief in technology. In this environment, puzzle pieces and images of catastrophe are legible as symbols, elucidating the intended contrasts between the two poles and referring to the artist's original concept: While the puzzle player only seems to concentrate so confidently on his game because the surrounding environment is in order, a disaster marks the exact point at which we lose a sure grip on our world and our lives.

In his installation, Draeger juxtaposes two videos. *Statistics* shows the almost meditative, peaceful and seemingly secure view from an aircraft window, while *Crash* portrays the history of air travel in terms of its catastrophes. Beginning with the Hindenburg disaster and documentary footage from the first and second World Wars, the video continues with quick-cut sequences of test crashes from the '60s and ends with the pure Hollywood fiction of countless aircrash films. In the progression from reality to manipulation to fiction, Draeger de- ciphers the structure of our ideas of reality. Hollywood's fiction is subconsciously conferred with great authenticity. It is its images that come into our consciousness when we read the dates of the century's 100 largest aircraft catastrophes, running past the "window" in film-credit form, from below to above. In this way, Draeger evokes a sense of what every passenger so easily forgets when he looks through the window at an endless sunny sky. At the same time, he buries the fundamentally positive representation of technology in the Zeppelin Museum itself: The myth of floating through the heavens is sharply contrasted with the question of technological failure.

This questioning is taken a step further in that the floor of the exhibition space is covered with almost two tons of puzzle pieces. Millions of image fragments, taken in the context of the medialization of reality, represent the immeasurable accumulation of increasingly similar images. On a haptic level, Draeger succeeds in deconstructing our concept of reality, based on our corresponding beliefs in the images and

in technology. In the context of this definition of reality, one must pay more and more attention to our mediality, and, because of the ever-increasing flood of external stimuli, information's extremely short life. Our images are assembled from ever smaller blocks of information, that are, however (according to the logic of news reports), to be consumed as a single, closed picture: The image of the world as a puzzle.

As the power of images grew, so did the limitations of information – not only to the news that could satisfy the requirements of largest masses possible, but also to the news that could attract the most attention. Both demands are met by catastrophe reports. News of this kind plays with our

den Nachgeschmack von Trauer oder Mitgefühl, d.h. ihre Rezeption funktioniert noch heute nach den gleichen Grundsätzen, die schon die Darstellungen bedrohlicher Visionen oder Landschaften zur Zeit des ausgehenden 18. Jahrhunderts kennzeichneten: Die Sicherheit des Betrachters vor dem Bild war die Grundlage für das ästhetische Genießen des Bildes. Zum anderen erscheint die Katastrophe in unserem Informationszeitalter als der einzige verbleibende Indikator, der uns überhaupt noch über eine Veränderung ins Bild zu setzen vermag.

Aus diesem Blickwinkel heraus betrachtet löst sich die vermeintlich konträre Stellung von Puzzle und Katastrophe auf und verwandelt sich in ein Symbol für jenes dekonstruierte bzw. dekonstruierbare Welt-Bild. Die Bilderflut generiert gerade keine Sicherheit, sondern konfrontiert uns immer wieder aufs Neue mit der Vertraubarkeit eben dieser Bilder. Genau diese Unsicherheit verspüren wir beim Betreten des über und über mit Puzzleteilen bedeckten Fußbodens des *Grenz-Raumes* im Zeppelin Museum. Auf den zentimeterdick aufgeschütteten, -zigmillionen kleinen Bildteilchen kann man physisch erfahren, wie die Überfülle an potentiellen Bildern den sicheren Stand raubt, so wie uns die immer gleichen, fast alltäglichen Katastrophenbilder den konkreten Bezug zu den Geschehnissen versperren: Die emotionale Halbwertzeit dieser Bilder ist kaum mehr meßbar. Zugleich erinnert die Oberfläche dieses «Bild-Sees» an ein aus großer Höhe aufgenommenes Trümmerfeld, wie es nach kriegerischen Auseinandersetzungen oder nach einem Erdbeben vorstellbar wäre und verweist so auf andere Arbeiten Draegers, in denen er Katastrophen quasi als Sandkastenspiele nachinszenierte.

Die Verbindung von Katastrophe und Puzzle läßt sich an einer Arbeit Draegers aus dem Jahr 1998 exemplarisch aufzeigen, die den Absturz des Fluges TWA 800 vor der amerikanischen Ostküste zum Ausgangspunkt hatte. Das Puzzle zeigt, wie die völlig zerstörte Maschine in einem Hangar aus den aus dem Meer gefischten Einzelteilen von Experten wieder zusammengebaut wird, um so den Hergang des Unglücks rekonstruieren zu können. Letzten Endes handelt es sich hierbei um ein riesiges 3-D-Puzzle, an dessen Ende jedoch nicht eigentlich das fertige Flugzeug steht, sondern die Wiedergewinnung jener trügerischen Sicherheit, die uns bei jedem Flug den Gedanken verdrängen hilft, daß auch wir Opfer einer solchen Katastrophe werden könnten.

In seiner Audio-Installation innerhalb der Teil-Rekonstruktion der LZ 129 Hindenburg beschäftigt sich Christoph Draeger noch auf andere Weise mit der physischen Reaktion auf die mögliche Erfahrung eines Absturzes und somit auch mit der Mehrschichtigkeit unserer Wahrnehmung. In der behaglichen 1:1-Nachbildung des Aufenthaltsraumes dröhnt alle 60 Minuten aus unsichtbaren Lautsprechern eine künstlerisch bearbeitete Version jener Tonsequenz

concept of and our search for security in two ways: On the one hand, the catastrophe becomes an aesthetic spectacle lacking the aftertaste of mourning or sympathy. This means its reception functions on the same principles that mark the representation of threatening visions of 18th-century landscapes. The secure position of the observer, in front of the image, acted as the foundation for aesthetic enjoyment of the observed object. On the other hand, in our information age, catastrophic news seems to be the only indicator that makes us aware of a change in image at all.

From this viewpoint, the seemingly contrasting positions of puzzle and catastrophe morph into a symbol of a deconstructed or deconstructable view of the world. The overflow of images does not generate security, but rather confronts us in new ways with the trustworthiness of these images. Exactly this insecurity is what Draeger forces us to feel when we step on the puzzle-piece-covered floor of the Zeppelin Museum's *Grenz-Raum* (Border Room). On the centimeter-thick layer of millions of tiny picture pieces, one can physically feel how the overflow of potential images robs us of our sense of security, just as the almost ordinary images of catastrophe block our concrete connection to the events themselves. The emotional half-life of these images is now barely measurable. At the same time, the surface of this "sea of images" reminds us of an aerial view of the ruins left by a war

aus dem Hollywood-Film *Die Hindenburg* (1975), mit der die Katastrophenszene und die Augenblicke vor dem Ausbrechen des Feuers unterlegt sind. Die Realität der Explosionsgeräusche und die Menschenstimmen werden so zum Katalysator, der den Film im Kopf des Publikums ablaufen läßt: Die museal rekonstruierte Luxuskabine des Luftschiffs mutiert zur Todeszelle, in der 35 Menschen den Tod fanden. In dieser Sound-Installation vermittelt Draeger unmittelbar die Ausweglosigkeit einer solchen Situation. Zwar sind die Museumsbesucher nicht durch ein Feuer bedroht, aber ersetzt wird diese Bedrohung durch die enorme Lautstärke der Installation. Die akustische Wucht der Explosionen läßt uns in gleicher Weise hektisch nach einem Fluchtweg suchen, wie dies wohl auch damals Passagiere und Besatzungsmitglieder vor der herannahenden Feuerwalze getan haben.

Mit dieser subjekt-gebundenen, imaginären Projektion verweist Draeger auf die Allgegenwart der Bilder, die uns heute «live» und meist im Rahmen einer Sondersendung ins Wohnzimmer geliefert werden.

1 **Tttttttiiiiiittttttaaaaaannnnnniiiiiicccccc**
Silkscreen, Edition R2/12, Geneva
2 **Crash**
B.I. Hengi, Nara Verlag 1993
3 **P.S.A. crash**
San Diego 1978, photo: Hans Wendt, Newsweek
Acrylic paint jet on jigsaw puzzle,
4000 pcs, 96 x 136 cm, 1999
4 **Sound effects disasters**
LP cover, Intercord/BBC records 1977

Die Katastrophe ist so nicht nur zum Paradigma der Welterfahrung im ausgehenden 20. Jahrhundert geworden, sondern, aufgrund ihrer medialen Ubiquität, zum Sinnbild jenes «rasenden Stillstandes» überhaupt (Paul Virilio). Die Größe einer Katastrophe wird heute nicht mehr aufgrund der Anzahl ihrer Opfer definiert, sondern anhand ihrer medialen Verwertbarkeit und der dadurch begründeten Tele-Präsenz, die uns mit eindrucksvollen Bildern den Schrecken als ästhetisches Erlebnis präsentiert.

or an earthquake. This view is reminiscent of Draeger's previous works, in which he constructs catastrophes as though he were constructing sandbox games.

The connection between catastrophe and puzzle is apparent almost exemplary in one of Draeger's 1998 works, based on the crash of TWA Flight 800 near the American east coast. The puzzle shows how experts rebuilt the completely destroyed aircraft from single parts fished out of the sea, in order to determine the origin of the disaster. The work concerns itself with nothing else but a huge three-dimensional puzzle at whose end there is no finished aircraft, but rather the sense of regained, but false security; a security that helps us forget that we could be the victims of such a disaster.

In his audio installation within the partial reconstruction of the LZ 129 Hindenburg, Christoph Draeger is concerned, in another way, with the physical reaction to the possible experience of a crash and the multilayered aspect of our perception. In the snug 1:1 reconstruction of the cabin, a version of the the audio sequence from the Hollywood film *The Hindenburg* (1975) plays every 60 minutes from hidden loudspeakers. These sounds are taken from scenes of the catastrophe itself as well as the few moments prior to the explosion. The reality of the explosive sounds and human voices becomes a catalyst that allows the film to run through the heads of museum visitors: The reconstructed cabin mutates into a death cell in which 35 people perished. In this sound installation, Draeger conveys the hopelessness of such a situation. While the museum visitor is not threatened by fire, the installation's enormous volume does become a threat. The explosion's acoustic power forces the visitor to quickly search for an escape, like the passengers and crew of the aircraft certainly must have done when faced with imminent destruction.

With this subject-bound, imaginary projection, Draeger points to the ubiquity of such images, which are delivered into our living rooms in the form of special news reports. At the end of the 20th century, catastrophe has not become a paradigm of world experience, but rather, because of its ubiquity in the media, the definitive image of "accelerating standstill" (Paul Virilio). The magnitude of a catastrophe is no longer measured by the number of its victims, but rather by its medial valuation and resulting telepresence – whose impressive images present us with horror as an aesthetic experience.

Translation: Kimberley Bradley, New York

The most beautiful disasters in the world

TWA 800
Acrylic paint jet on jigsaw puzzle,
7500 pcs, 110 x 260 cm, 1998

Ramstein
Acrylic paint jet on jigsaw puzzle,
4000 pcs, 96 x 136 cm, 1999

Untitled
Drawing, 30 x 40 cm, Brussels 1992

Puzzled (detail)
Kulturhaus Rosengarten, Grüsch, 1998

ICE 886: the great German train disaster
Acrylic paint jet on jigsaw puzzle,
8000 pcs, 136 x 192 cm, 1999

Critical distance
Installation view, ADO Gallery, Antwerp
1993

Hurricane Andrew
Acrylic paint jet on jigsaw puzzle,
8000 pcs, 136 x 192 cm, 1993

Teneriffa 1977 (largest aircrash ever)
Reims 1918
Mount St. Helens
All acrylic paint jet on jigsaw puzzle,
4000 pcs, 96 x 136 cm, 1993

Tornado, Kissimee, Florida
Acrylic paint jet on jigsaw puzzle,
4000 pcs, 96 x 136 cm, 1999

L. A. Earthquake
Acrylic paint jet on jigsaw puzzle,
4000 pcs, 136 x 96 cm, 1993

Tornado, Spencer, South Dakota
Acrylic paint jet on jigsaw puzzle,
8000 pcs, 136 x 192 cm, 1999

Hurricane David, Dominican Republic
Acrylic paint jet on jigsaw puzzle,
7500 pcs, 110 x 260 cm, 1999

Flood, Seoul, Corea
Acrylic paint jet on jigsaw puzzle,
8000 pcs, 136 x 192 cm, 1999

Catastrophe #1
Acrylic paint jet on pvc, 220 x 330 cm
Model: 100m²
Trash, plaster, wood, pigments etc
Brussels, 1993–94

Duel, video stills
Video, 8 min, 1999
(Henry Fonda and Charles Bronson
in *Once Upon a Time in the West*,
Sergio Leone, 1968)

Action//Time//Vision (Alternative TV)

Orchard Gallery, Derry, 1999

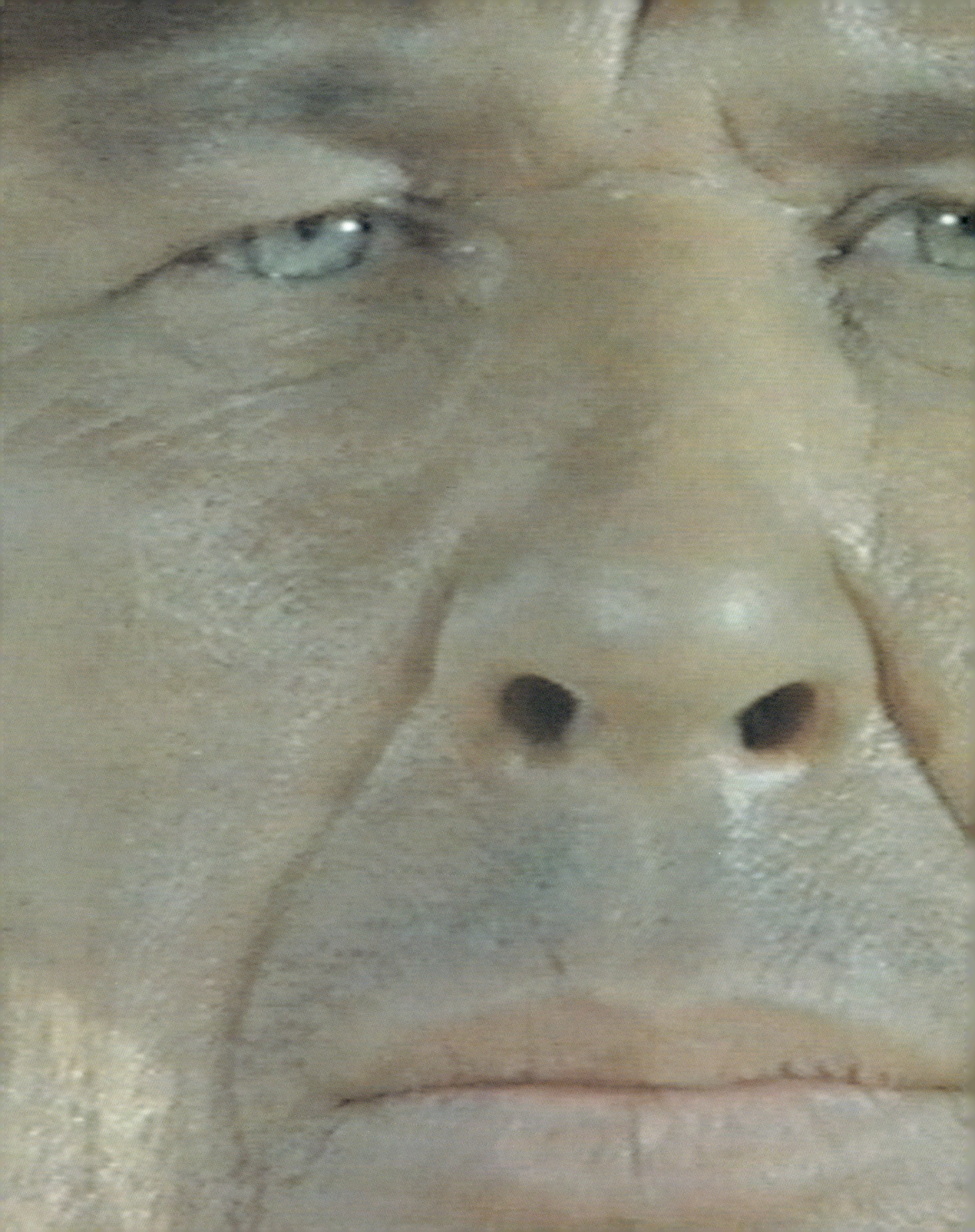

Good Old Douglas Bader, Bad Old Andreas Baader
Padraig Timoney

It's curious in a way that *Trinity* and *Duel*, two of Christoph Draeger's new works presented in Derry, take as their original material showdowns from two classic Sergio Leone westerns – *The Good, the Bad and the Ugly* and *Once Upon a Time in the West*. The reworking of the chosen sequences, perhaps unwittingly, initializes relationships to a local penchant, at least among the older, male population, for the Western as type to hold an invigorated mythological status. I have previously felt that Northern and Southern Ireland were indeed the Western lands; the ideal for living supplied by Sunday afternoon's TV films, the fiction of Louis L'Amour, JT Edson, and all that "a man's gotta do what a man's gotta do" stuff. It was enough to say that, for example, *High Noon* was a great film, in order to acknowledge an appreciation of righteous behavior and the inevitable victory over things sent to test it. Only partly occupied by religion, mythological capacity was presented with Hollywood's version of the New World, *Amerikay*. Perhaps this was immediately interesting given the number of Irish emigrants who had made their way to the Wild West, refugees from hunger and poverty – films supplied the stories what might have happened to them. Conveniently, as with most mythology, the idea of cathartic confrontation with destiny happened somewhere else and to someone fictional, removed from present time, situation and application. In the video works of *Duel*, *Trinity* and *If six was five*, the shootings, detached but remembered as metonymous of the whole film, are seen as resulting from basic mythological themes/human motivations – Greed, Duty, Law and Order, Revenge – all played out at the "moment of truth".

Guter alter Douglas Bader, böser alter Andreas Baader
Padraig Timoney

In gewisser Weise ist es kurios, daß *Trinity* und *Duel,* zwei der neuen, in Derry vorgestellten Arbeiten von Christoph Draeger, als Ausgangsmaterial Kraftproben aus zwei klassischen Western Sergio Leones entnehmen – *The Good, the Bad and the Ugly* und *Once upon a Time in the West*. Die Überarbeitung der ausgewählten Sequenzen erschließt, vielleicht unbeabsichtigt, Verbindungen zu einer hiesigen Schwäche, zumindest unter der älteren, männlichen Bevölkerung, für den Western als Typus, der einen ausgeprägten mythologischen Status hat. Ich hatte früher das Gefühl, daß Nord- und Südirland in der Tat die Western-Länder seien; ein Lebensideal, das von Sonntagnachmittag-Fernsehfilmen geliefert wird, von den Erzählungen Louis L'Amours, JT Edsons und all diesen «ein Mann muß tun, was ein Mann tun muß»-Geschichten. Es genügte zu sagen, daß zum Beispiel *High Noon* ein großartiger Film sei, um eine Würdigung rechtschaffenen Verhaltens sowie den unausweichlichen Triumph über die zur Glaubensprüfung entsandten Dinge zu bekennen. Nur teilweise von Religion besetzt, wurde mythologischer Gehalt mittels Hollywoods Version der Neuen Welt, *Amerikay*, vorgestellt. Vielleicht war das unmittelbar interessant angesichts der Anzahl von irischen Emigranten, die sich in den Wilden Westen aufgemacht hatten, Flüchtlinge vor Hunger und Armut – Filme lieferten die Geschichten darüber, was ihnen zugestoßen sein mochte. Glücklicherweise trug sich die kathartische Konfrontation mit dem Schicksal, wie es mit den meisten Mythologien der Fall ist, woanders zu und betraf eine fiktive Person, die so entfernt von der heutigen Zeit, Situation und Gültigkeit war wie alle Götter auf dem Olymp. In den Videoarbeiten *Duel*, *Trinity* und *If six was five* werden die Schießereien – aus dem Zusammenhang gerissen, aber als Metonymie für den gesamten Film erinnert – als Resultate elementarer mythologischer Themen/menschlicher Motivationen betrachtet: Gier, Pflicht, Gesetz und Ordnung, Rache, allesamt im «Moment der Wahrheit» ausgespielt. Die Bereitstellung und Anerkennung von Mythologie (als Unterhaltung) bleibt weitverbreitet, ist aber auf eine bestimmte Funktion beschränkt, ein Dampfablassen oder eine Angleichung an ein paar konstruierte Vorstellungen über das Wesen der Menschheit. Obwohl die fiktiven Western-Charaktere einen besonderen Platz in der hiesigen Vorstellungswelt einnehmen, beweisen die Schwierigkeiten, die mit der Präsentation einer anderen Arbeit Draegers, der Serie *Citizens of Derry* verbunden waren, daß eine vorsätzliche Vermischung von Fiktion und Realität mit den Sensibilitäten der hiesigen Öffentlichkeit gegenüber ihrer eigenen Identifikation mit den Medien in Konflikt gerät, wie auch mit der Distanz, in welcher die beliebtesten filmischen Mythologien gehalten werden. Und sie zeigen auch, in Gegenwart der beson-

The supply and appreciation of mythology (as entertainment) is widespread, but it is limited to a certain function, a letting off of steam, or an alignment with some constructed idea of the essence of humanity. Although Western fictional characters seem to hold a special place in the local imagination, the difficulties inherent in presenting a different work, the series *Citizens of Derry,* show that an intended confusion of the fiction and the real entangles with the sensitivities of the local public towards their own media identification, and the distance at which the favorites of filmic mythology are kept. And, in the presence of the specialized reality that a world famous "trouble-spot" becomes, shows where upon the scale of real importance Hollywood's mythology occurs.

For reasons of security, *Citizens of Derry* was shown inside the Orchard Gallery, although it had been envisaged as a public artwork, intended for above the entrance of the Orchard Gallery. It was felt that there was the possibility of trouble, even serious public disturbance, if the photos were just dropped into a public situation without contextualisation. Where could the difficulty lie? Taken from a 1972 *Life Magazine* feature on Northern Ireland, the Bogside and Free Derry, (names which had become famous throughout the media and almost become household), five photographs of people wearing masks, balaclavas and berets were overprinted with names of well known actors Clint Eastwood, Charles Bronson, Geena Davis, Robert de Niro and John Travolta. Not characters' names, inscribing them as related to particular films, but actors' names, beings who become others than themselves, in order to pretend action. Their names are as famous as their faces. When faces are covered up simply to avoid arrest for belonging to illegal organizations, their identity is also automatically subsumed into a group, they become soldiers, indivisible. Recognized as a member, in a context – by implication, a whole population behind it, this person can be someone, everyone and no-one.

There is a difference between entertainment and actuality. Draeger makes the point that in one sense they can be called anything, as their hiding leaves them vessels for description, for special purpose. Given the proclivity of the media to be never more than shortcoming, as associated with psychosis and criminality, that's how the pro-

2

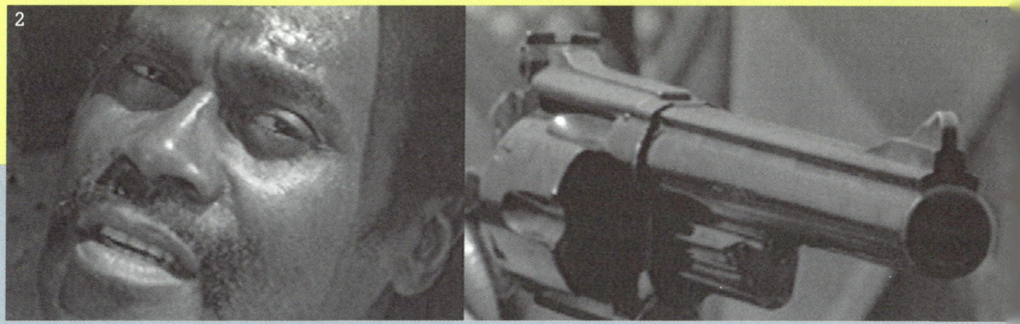

deren Realität, zu der eine weltberühmte "Problemzone" unweigerlich wird, an welcher Stelle auf der Skala wirklicher Bedeutung die Mythologie Hollywoods erscheint.

Aus Sicherheitsgründen wurde *Citizens of Derry* im Inneren der Orchard Gallery gezeigt, obwohl die Arbeit als ein öffentliches Kunstwerk im Außenraum vorgesehen war. Man hatte das Gefühl, daß Ärger oder gar ernsthafte öffentliche Unruhen nicht auszuschließen wären, wenn man die Photos einfach einer öffentlichen Situation ohne Kontextualisierung überließe. Wo könnte die Schwierigkeit liegen? Einer *Life Magazine*-Reportage von 1971 über Nordirland, die Bogside und Free Derry entnommen (Namen, die durch die Medien berühmt wurden und fast überall geläufig sind), wurden fünf Photographien von Leuten mit Masken, Balaklavamützen und Baretten mit den Namen von bekannten Schauspielern überdruckt – Clint Eastwood, Charles Bronson, Geena Davis, Robert de Niro und John Travolta. Nicht die Namen der Charaktere, welche sie in Verbindung mit bestimmten Filmen bringen würden, sondern die Namen der Schauspieler, jener Wesen, die jemand anders als sie selbst werden, um eine Handlung zu simulieren. So berühmt wie ihre Gesichter. Wenn Gesichter bedeckt sind – schlicht um Festnahme wegen Zugehörigkeit zu einer illegalen Organisation zu vermeiden –, wird dabei auch die Identität des Individuums automatisch einer Gruppe zugeordnet, wird zum Soldaten, nicht mehr unterscheidbar. Als ein Mitglied und in einem Kontext registriert, ist diese Person, hinter der implizit eine ganze Bevölkerung steht, zugleich jemand, jeder und niemand.

Es gibt einen Unterschied zwischen Unterhaltung und Wirklichkeit. Draeger macht deutlich, daß sie in mancher Hinsicht als alles mögliche bezeichnet werden können, da ihr Verstecken sie zu Gefäßen für Beschreibung, für bestimmte Zwecke macht. Und daß angesichts der Tendenz der Medien, nie mehr als unzulänglich zu sein, die Befürworter programmatischer politischer Gewalt dem Rest der Welt als assoziiert mit Psychose und Kriminalität vorgeführt werden. Damit verflochten ist eine unerbetene und stillschweigende Botschaft, persönlich und doch anonym: So wird deine Gewalt vom Rest der Welt aufgenommen. Und damit alle Gewalt. Der Boden, dieser heimische Boden, ist somit auch ein Feld, wo es gilt, von den Medien ein akkurates und einfühlsames Porträt zu erreichen; man denke an den umfassenden Protest und die Hungerstreiks der Republikaner in den 80ern und deren Ziel, den Gefangenenstatus als politisch anstatt kriminell zu definieren. Die Identifizierung der fotografierten Personen mit Schauspielern könnte den Schluß nahelegen, daß die Aktivitäten erfunden seien. Oder daß deren Haltung gestellt sei. Oder daß sich mit den Namen selbst Gangster, Cowboys, Kriminelle und Psychopathen verbinden – Assoziationen, die die

ponents of programmatic political violence are represented to the rest of the world. Entwined with this is an unsolicited and tacit address, personal and yet anonymous, that this is how your violence appears to the rest of the world. And by implication, all violence. The ground, this home ground, is then also a field where the goal is to secure an accurate and sensitive media portrayal; one remembers the Republican blanket protest and hunger strikes of the 1980's and their object of fixing the status of prisoners as political and not criminal. The identification of the photographs, with actors, could be seen to imply that their activity was fictional. Or that the attitude is put on. Or that the names themselves are connected with gangsters, cowboys, criminals, psychopaths – not an association that the represented would want to promote, figuring as it would, an ignorance of the reality that organizational violence was supposedly ideologically sponsored. To a media and politically literate population, the trivialisation of the images and the proponents of public disobedience there figured is, if so taken, a seriously willful misreading and playfulness that threatens to chip some of the classicised patina off their own legendary struggle. It seems impossible to "lighten up" this history, these figures – too much has been lost, sacrificed – purposeful irony, for example, in this area could only be achieved with extreme circumspection.

The attempt to address the relationship between local sensitivity and media-products (sprung from the same streets) which can become useful and thought-provoking material is necessarily complex. But for clear implication of a gnarled intentionality, space for consideration of everything needs first to be established. The gallery affords time, space, sanction; this is an artwork and not a thoughtlessly provocative appropriation of the easy equation – violence is relevant here. The gallery surrounds works with the auratic of protection and lineage; the public enters the space to see things and therefore the responsibility for what they take from it is eventually down to their own volition. Appearing there contextualised by Draeger's other operative mediations, the importance of looking further into the surface-only operations of the mass-media is generated by the opening of a locally meaningful intervention.

The history of violence inevitably recreates its own legends, heroes, villains, cowards, losers, great and disastrous days and nights. The mythic as contemporaneous with, and drawn from, sustained programs of violence are not accessible to the greater part of the media-world's audience. Localized and protected, these mythicalisations are obviously particular to each of all "different sides", and so remain part of the identity of oppositionality within a particularized and exclusive cordon. This represents an inturning audience restriction which would be anathema to mass-media phenomena with general appeal, such as football or the most popular television shows. The maintenance of these legends is effected in a similarly localised, low-end manner; gable-end murals, song, word of mouth, small circulation press. Continued isolation of the situations' reality is also effectuated by the mass-media's faulty memory of the ongoing troubles' original impetus. The vaunting of

3

Dargestellten nicht würden befördern wollen, da dies als Verkennung der Tatsache erscheinen könnte, daß die Gewalt von Organisationen vermeintlich ideologisch sei. Für eine politisch gebildete und mediensensibilisierte Bevölkerung bedeutet die Trivialisierung der Bilder und damit der dargestellten Befürworter öffentlichen Ungehorsams – versteht man sie so – eine ernsthafte, vorsätzliche Mißdeutung und Verspieltheit, die etwas von der klassisch gewordenen Patina ihres eigenen legendären Kampfes zum Abplatzen zu bringen droht. Es scheint unmöglich, diese Geschichte, diese Figuren «aufzuhellen» – zu viel wurde verloren, geopfert. Eine beabsichtigte Ironie beispielsweise auf diesem Gebiet könnte nur mit extremer Umsicht erreicht werden. Der Versuch, das Verhältnis zwischen hiesiger Sensibilität und Medienprodukten (die von den gleichen Straßen herstammen) anzusprechen, was nützliches und gedankenanregendes Material hervorbringen kann, ist zwangsläufig komplex. Aber für die klare Implikation einer verformten Intentionalität muß zuerst Raum für eine Berücksichtigung aller Aspekte geschaffen werden. Die Galerie gewährt Zeit, Raum und Sanktionierung; es handelt sich um ein Kunstwerk und nicht um eine gedankenlos provokative Aneignung der einfachen Gleichung – Gewalt ist relevant hier vor Ort. Die Galerie umgibt die Arbeiten mit einer Aura von Schutz und Einbettung. Das Publikum betritt den Ort, um sich etwas anzusehen und übernimmt damit eine freiwillige Verantwortung dafür, was letztlich von dort mitgenommen wird. Indem die Arbeit hier im Kontext von Draegers anderen Eingriffen und Vermittlungen erscheint, wird die Bedeutung eines tiefergehenden Blicks auf die Oberflächen-Operationen der Massenmedien durch die Eröffnung einer lokal bedeutsamen Intervention unterstrichen.

Die Geschichte der Gewalt erfindet sich unvermeidlich immer wieder ihre eigenen Legenden, Helden, Verbrecher, Feiglinge, Verlierer und verhängnisvollen Tage und Nächte. Das Mythische als Zeitgenosse und zugleich Resultat andauernder programmatischer Gewalt ist dem Großteil des Publikums der Medienwelt nicht zugäng-

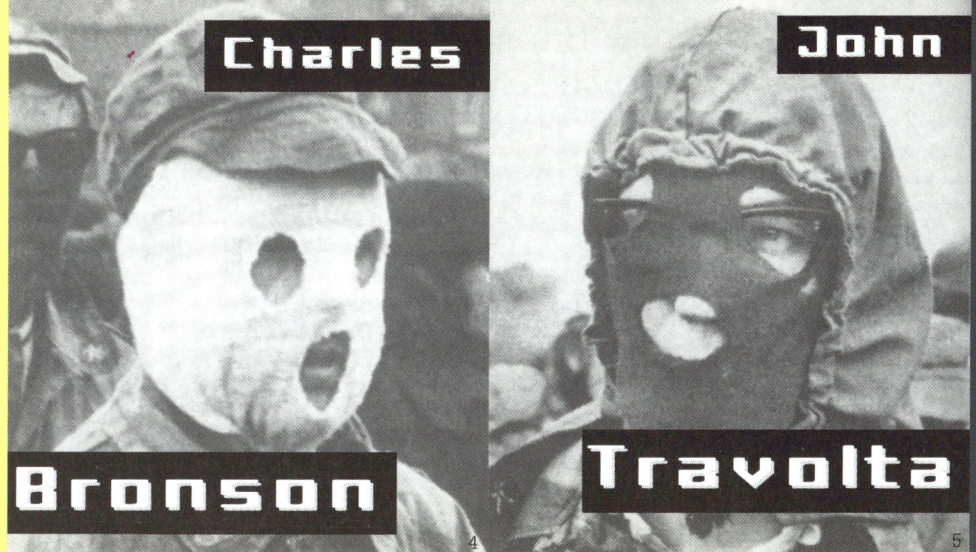

legitimacy through ideology now seems, given the emergence of Third Way politics in the West, somehow anachronistic, atavistic – but the photographs do come from a period when the world sort of knew generally the motivations of the political left and right. In that era, the idea of international solidarity meant that the aforementioned mythologies were not solely localized, but contributed to a language and atmosphere of opposition that was widespread through the world.

Draeger's *Black and white room,* a reconstruction of a 1970's sitting room, surrounds the viewer with constant points of referral – like the major particles of an atomic structure, the type of chair, lamp, record player, and image-carriers on the wall and floor are characteristic of widely distributed designs of consumer durables from that particular period. The illusion trades on the typicality of the props, not their specificity, as the schematic means of describing a time capsule. The room is set up to watch TV, listen to one 45' record (*Action, Time, Vision* by *Alternative TV,* from 1977) or to look at its decorative panels, images of Stammheim prison and Andreas Baader's prison record player (a copy from Gerhard Richters' series on RAF terrorists, *18. Oktober 1977*). Schematic, gestalt provision, metonymy, whatever – the re-creation of a particular situation is made formally expressive by its black-and-whiteness, coinciding with Draeger's own recollection of the era. The only color is provided by the urgent montage of

lich. Lokalisiert und geschützt finden diese Mythologisierungen offenbar auf jeder der «verschiedenen Seiten» statt und bleiben damit Teil der Identität von Oppositionalität innerhalb eines spezifizierten und exklusiven Kordons. Dies stellt eine sich nach innen wendende Publikumsbeschränkung dar, die ein Greuel wäre für Massenmedienphänomene wie etwa Fußball oder die beliebtesten Fernsehsendungen. Die Aufrechterhaltung dieser Legenden wird in einer ähnlich lokal begrenzten, einfachen Weise betrieben: Wandgemälde, Songs, Mundpropaganda, Presse in kleineren Auflagen. Fortgesetzte Isolierung der Realität der Situation wird auch dadurch bewirkt, daß die Massenmedien die ursprüngliche Motivation für die anhaltenden Probleme nur fehlerhaft erinnern. Sich mit durch Ideologie bewiesener Rechtmäßigkeit zu brüsten, scheint heute, angesichts des Aufkommens der Politik des Dritten Wegs im Westen, irgendwie anachronistisch, atavistisch – die Photographien stammen jedoch aus einer Zeit, als die Welt die Motivationen der politischen Linken und Rechten eigentlich im allgemeinen kannte. In dieser Ära bedeute-

te die Idee von internationaler Solidarität, daß die zuvor erwähnten Mythologien nicht lokal begrenzt waren, sondern zu einer Sprache und einer oppositionellen Atmosphäre beitrugen, die in der ganzen Welt verbreitet waren.

Draegers *Black and white room,* eine Rekonstruktion eines Aufenthaltsraums der 70er Jahre, umgibt den Besucher mit konstanten Bezugspunkten – wie Hauptbestandteile einer Atomstruktur. Die Art von Stuhl, Lampe, Plattenspieler und Bildträger an der Wand und auf dem Boden sind charakteristisch für weitverbreitetes Design von Konsumgütern dieser Zeit. Die Illusion macht sich die Typenhaftigkeit der Requisiten, nicht deren spezifische Eigenschaften, als schematisches Mittel zur Beschreibung einer Zeitkapsel zunutze. Der Raum ist zum Fernsehen eingerichtet, zum Hören einer Schallplatte (*Action, Time, Vision* von *Alternative TV,* von 1977) oder zur Betrachtung der dekorativen Tafeln, Bilder vom Stammheim-Gefängnis und von Andreas Baaders Gefängnisplattenspieler (eine Kopie aus der Serie von Gerhard Richter über die RAF-Terroristen, *18. Oktober 1977*). Schematisch, Gestaltlieferung, Metonymie, was immer – die Wiederherstellung einer bestimmten Situation wird durch ihren Schwarz-Weiß-Charakter formal ausdrucksvoll, was mit Draegers eigenen Erinnerungen an diese Ära übereinstimmt. Die einzige Farbe wird von den eindringlichen Montagen von Flugzeugentführungen, Terroristenalarmen, fotogenem/radikalem Schick und Schutzmaßnahmen der Fluglinien geliefert, die *Dial H.I.S.T.O.R.Y* von Johan Grimonprez im Fernsehmonitor abspielt. Fundamental für die Freizeitpark-Erfahrung der Wieder-Darstellung ist die halluzinatorische Verdichtung der Aneignung – eine Überladung an vermittelten Berichten in ahistorischer Zeitfolge. Die von dieser Zeitkapsel produzierte Nostalgie für eine Epoche, in der es im Fernsehen nichts als Terrorismus zu sehen gab, wird als ein Produkt einer lückenhaften und korrumpierten Erinnerung offenbart und als ein ernsthafter Hinweis auf die Art und Weise, wie die Medien dort ereignisgebundene, biographische Markierungen vornahmen. Ich erinnere mich an die schwierigen frühen 70er Jahre – Baader-Meinhof,

hijackings, terrorist alerts, photogenic/radical chic, and airline precautions that Johan Grimonprez's *Dial H.I.S.T.O.R.Y* plays on the TV. Fundamental to the theme-park experience of the re-presentation is the hallucinatory condensation of appropriations – an overload of mediated reports in an ahistorical time-sequence. Produced by this time-capsule, nostalgia for a time when there was nothing on TV but terrorism is revealed as a product of a partial and corrupted memory, and a genuine indication of the media's insertion of event-related biographical markers. I remember the troubled early seventies – Baader-Meinhof, Fidel, Yasser Arafat, Moshe Dayan, OPEC, the PLO, UDA and the Provos. Names coming out of the blanket of the media to introduce something to the physiology and psychology of a child as it begins to apprehend the world around it. Only the older generation could blame names, could hold a judgment. To the young person, the child, these names' repetition must be part of growing into the world, a warmth and motherly fondness growing at their mention. The outcome of salient-based memory, and the nostalgia is for a world like childhood, with clearer definitions – a memory of basic lumps. It's against my nature to object to these things. To myself and others of Draeger's generation, nostalgia is taken as a refuge from the idea that the world has changed, that the ideologically rigid has seemed to disappear; Cuba is a museum, and we never understood the collapse of the Berlin Wall in the same way that an older generation did. Ideological violence was bilaterally aligned in those times, smaller in size than the overhanging threat of the superpowers' arsenals. Is the break-up of the larger confrontation related to the decay of ideology into today's I.D.ology? And what's a bomb these days but a press release?

Whether or not from the idea that children of the media-age, nurtured with a backdrop of famously violent names, cannot get beyond the siren call of the nostalgic, there is no overt criticism of programmatic violence in Draeger's work; perhaps a futile operation shown in his treatment of images of natural disasters, earthquakes etc. – but who would be criticized? God? Violence inscribed as inevitable and moreover unpredictable – approximating it to the natural? The register of images and sources from the media, both reportage and filmic, is held to be an operation of surfaces, spectacularisations made fluid and interchangeable. The idea of emphatic involvement, "what it would really be like", is taken as a by-product of this frontality, an imaginatively sponsored delving. Is there a slipping of ability to discern the difference, zapping across the visual cata-

Fidel, Yassir Arafat, Moshe Dayan, OPEC, die PLO, UDA und die Provos. Aus der Mediendecke quellende Namen, welche die Physiologie und Psychologie eines Kindes in etwas einführten, während es begann, die Welt um sich herum zu begreifen. Nur die ältere Generation konnte Namen mit Schuld verbinden, konnte ein Urteil fällen. Für den jungen Menschen, das Kind, mußte die Wiederholung dieser Namen Teil des Indie-Welt-Wachsens sein, ihrer Erwähnung entströmte eine Wärme und mütterliche Zuneigung. Das Resultat einer Erinnerung, die sich auf Auffälliges gründet, und die Nostalgie gehören in eine Welt wie die der Kindheit, mit klareren Definitionen – eine Erinnerung elementarer Brocken. Es widerstrebt mir von Natur aus, mich gegen diese Dinge zu verwahren. Ich und andere aus Draegers Generation suchen in der Nostalgie eine Zuflucht vor der Idee, daß sich die Welt verändert hat, daß die ideologische Starre zu verschwinden scheint. Kuba ist ein Museum, und wir haben den Fall der Berliner Mauer nie in derselben Weise verstanden wie eine ältere Generation dies tat. Ideologische Gewalt war damals bilateral ausgerichtet und von geringerem Ausmaß als die überhängende Bedrohung der Waffenarsenale der Supermächte. Ist das Aufbrechen der größeren Konfrontation mit dem Verfall der Ideologie zur heutigen I.D.ologie verbunden? Und was ist eine Bombe heutzutage außer einer Pressemitteilung?

Ob oder ob nicht von der Vorstellung hergeleitet, daß Kinder des Medienzeitalters, die mit berühmten gewalttätigen Namen genährt wurden, nicht jenseits des Sirenengesangs der Nostalgie gelangen können – jedenfalls findet sich in Draegers Arbeiten keine übermäßige Kritik an programmati- scher Gewalt. Vielleicht ein vergebliches Unterfangen, offenbart in seinem Umgang mit Bildern von Naturkatastrophen, Erdbeben usw. – wer sollte dort auch kritisiert werden? Gott? Gewalt, die als unvermeidlich und zudem unberechenbar verzeichnet wird – in Annäherung an die Natur? Das Register an Bildern und Quellen aus den Medien, sowohl in Form von Reportagen als auch Filmen, wird für einen Vorgang von Oberflächen gehalten; Sensationalisierungen werden fließend und austauschbar. Die Vorstellung vom emphatischen Beteiligtsein – «wie es wirklich wäre» – wird als Nebenprodukt dieser Konfrontierung hingenommen, ein phantasievoll unterstütztes Eintauchen. Entgleitet beim Zappen durch den visuellen Katalog des Fernsehens die Fähigkeit, den Unterschied zwischen Realität und Fiktion zu erkennen? Wenn Desaster nur im Fernsehen sichtbar sind, nachdem sie von einer Crew draußen vor Ort eingespeist wurden, und in der gleichen Weise erscheinen wie ein Film, wie real sind sie dann? Findet die Aufführung des Spiels überhaupt statt? Und wie indirekt kann man werden?

logue of television, between fiction and the real? If the disastrous is only on television, fed in from an outside crew on location, but appearing the same way that a film would, how real is it? Is the game show happening at all? And how vicarious can you get?

Draeger, in his admission of never being aggressor nor victim of a media-worthy violence, acts out the complications of "identifying with" in the video piece *Feel lucky, punk??!*. Taking the media for material, and underscoring its artificiality, Draeger's set-up situations aim to allow us to feel involved in the original action, by intelligently intervening to change the formal flow of the original bit. Reshooting robbery scenes from famous films with himself and friends as the protagonists, then intercutting these takes into the play of the original movie, the artist makes obvious the third-hand quality of identification; aping something, a well-known sequence, that never really happened. Except that it did happen once – in Hollywood. The subject of identification, with whatever bastardized mythology available, seems related to a crossing of art's often-quoted idea of telling the rest of us what life is about with the imagination that experience of violence and its adrenaline is necessary for feeling really alive. Bone like chrome on ultra-frictionless joints, the feeling of moving above the surface of the earth, real material become magic in the hands, become symbolic. This exemplary description of a mediated distance from enervated reality, seen through art, reminds me of the visual aesthetics of violence itself, remembering petrol bombs' beautiful brightest orange flame jumping on the gray surface of an RUC land-rover on a misty, gray, lightless damp afternoon in the North. And snipers and bomb scares articulating the body and relation to space in a way that sculptures' theoretics have always talked about – it suddenly and absolutely matters.

1,4,5,6 **Citizens of Derry**
Bubble jet prints, 70 x 110 cm, 1999

2 **If six was five,** video still
Video 1 min 45 sec, 1999

3 **Three planes exploding in the desert**
Still photograph for *Dial H.I.S.T.O.R.Y.*,
Johan Grimonprez 1997

4 Last scene from **Duel**
3-channel video installation, Orchard Gallery, Derry 1999

Douglas Bader was a legendary fighter pilot for the RAF (Royal Air Force) in the 2nd World War. He lost his legs in a crash and then continued to fly missions after learning to walk on tin legs. This English hero is the subject of *Reach for the Sky*, a typical Sunday afternoon British classic film.

Andreas Baader was one of the most notorious terrorist of the RAF (Red Army Fraction), in the 1970's in Germany. On October 18 1977, Baader allegedly committed suicide, together with his prison mates Jan Caarl Raspe and Gudrun Ensslin, in the high security prison of Stuttgart Stammheim.

Während Draeger zugibt, weder Angreifer noch Opfer eines Gewaltakts zu sein, der den Medien würdig wäre, spielt er die Komplikationen des Identifizierens in Videoarbeiten wie *Feel lucky, punk??!* vor. Draegers inszenierte Situationen, in denen die Medien als Ausgangsmaterial dienen und dessen Künstlichkeit unterstrichen wird, zielen darauf ab, uns das Gefühl eines Eingebundenseins in die ursprüngliche Situation zu ermöglichen. Auf intelligente Weise wird in den formalen Fluß des originalen Stück Films eingegriffen und dieser verändert. Indem er Überfallszenen aus berühmten Filmen mit sich selbst und Freunden als den Protagonisten nachdreht, diese Aufnahmen dann in den Ablauf des Originalfilms hineinschneidet, offenbart der Künstler die Dritte-Hand-Qualität von Identifikationen. Er ahmt etwas nach, eine bekannte Handlungssequenz, die nie wirklich stattgefunden hat. Außer daß sie doch einmal stattgefunden hat – in Hollywood. Das Thema der Identifikation – mit welcher auch immer gerade erhältlichen verfälschten Mythologie – scheint verbunden zu sein mit einer Art Kreuzung aus der vielzitierten Idee der Kunst, dem Rest der Welt mitzuteilen, was der Sinn des Lebens sei, und der Vorstellung, daß die Erfahrung von Gewalt und das damit verbundene Adrenalin notwendig sei, um sich wirklich lebendig zu fühlen. Knochen wie Chrom auf ultrareibungslosen Gelenken, das Gefühl, sich über die Erdoberfläche zu bewegen, reales Material wird magisch in den Händen, wird symbolisch. Diese beispielhafte Beschreibung einer vermittelten Distanz von abgeschwächter Realität, gesehen durch die Kunst, erinnert mich an die visuelle Ästhetik von Gewaltakten selbst, an die schöne, helle, orange Flamme von Benzinbomben, die an einem nebligen, grauen, lichtlosen, feuchten Nachmittag im Norden von der grauen Oberfläche eines Landrovers der nordirischen Polizei springt. Und Heckenschützen und Bombendrohungen artikulieren den Körper und das Verhältnis zum Raum in einer Weise, wie sie von den Theorien zur Skulptur immer beschrieben wurden – als von plötzlicher und absoluter Bedeutung.

Übersetzung: Sabine Russ

Douglas Bader war ein legendärer Kampfpilot der Royal Air Force (RAF) im 2.Weltkrieg. Er verlor beide Beine bei einem Absturz, flog aber weiterhin Einsätze, nachdem er gelernt hatte, auf Prothesen zu gehen. Dieser englische Kriegsheld ist die Hauptfigur in *Reach for the Sky*, einem klassischen britischen Sonntagnachmittagsdrama.

Andreas Baader war im Deutschland der 70er Jahre einer der gefürchtetsten Terroristen der Roten Armee Fraktion (RAF). Am 18. Oktober 1977 beging er in seiner Zelle im Hochsicherheitsgefängnis Stuttgart Stammheim angeblich Selbstmord, zusammen mit den RAF-Mitgliedern Jan Caarl Raspe und Gudrun Ensslin.

Action//Time//Vision
Installationview (The Duel)
Orchard Gallery, Derry 1999
3-channel laser disk video
installation, stereo

Action: Trinity
(The Good, the Bad and the Ugly, Sergio Leone, 1966)

Time: If six was five
(Dirty Harry, Don Siegel, 1971)

Vision: Duel
(Once Upon a Time in the West, Sergio Leone, 1968)

"Keep your loving brother happy"

**Black & white room –
Memories of terror from a safe distance**
Installation views Orchard Gallery, Derry
1999
70's plastic furniture, turntable, painting, carpet, lamp, TV

The installation features the following works:

Stuttgart-Stammheim
Acrylic paint jet on carpet, 220 x 330 cm, 1999

Dial H.I.S.T.O.R.Y., Johan Grimonprez, 1997
Video VHS, 68 min, (copy), 1999

Untitled, from the series **18. Oktober 1977,**
Gerhard Richter, 1987
(Andreas Baaders' turntable)
Acrylic paint jet on canvas, 66 x 87 cm, (copy), 1999

Action Time Vision, Alternative TV, 1977
Single on turntable, 45 rpm, 2 min 30

37

38

Citizens of Derry
at the opening

Citizens of Derry
Installation view Orchard Gallery, Derry 1999
Bubble jet prints, 70 x 110 cm

The library: conflict research center
Installation views Orchard Gallery, Derry 1999
ca 60 books and magazines on terrorism,
inflatable chairs, tables

Another island: my holidays in Corsica
Installation view Orchard Gallery, Derry 1999
Slideprojector, 40 slides
Photos: Jules Spinatsch, 1997

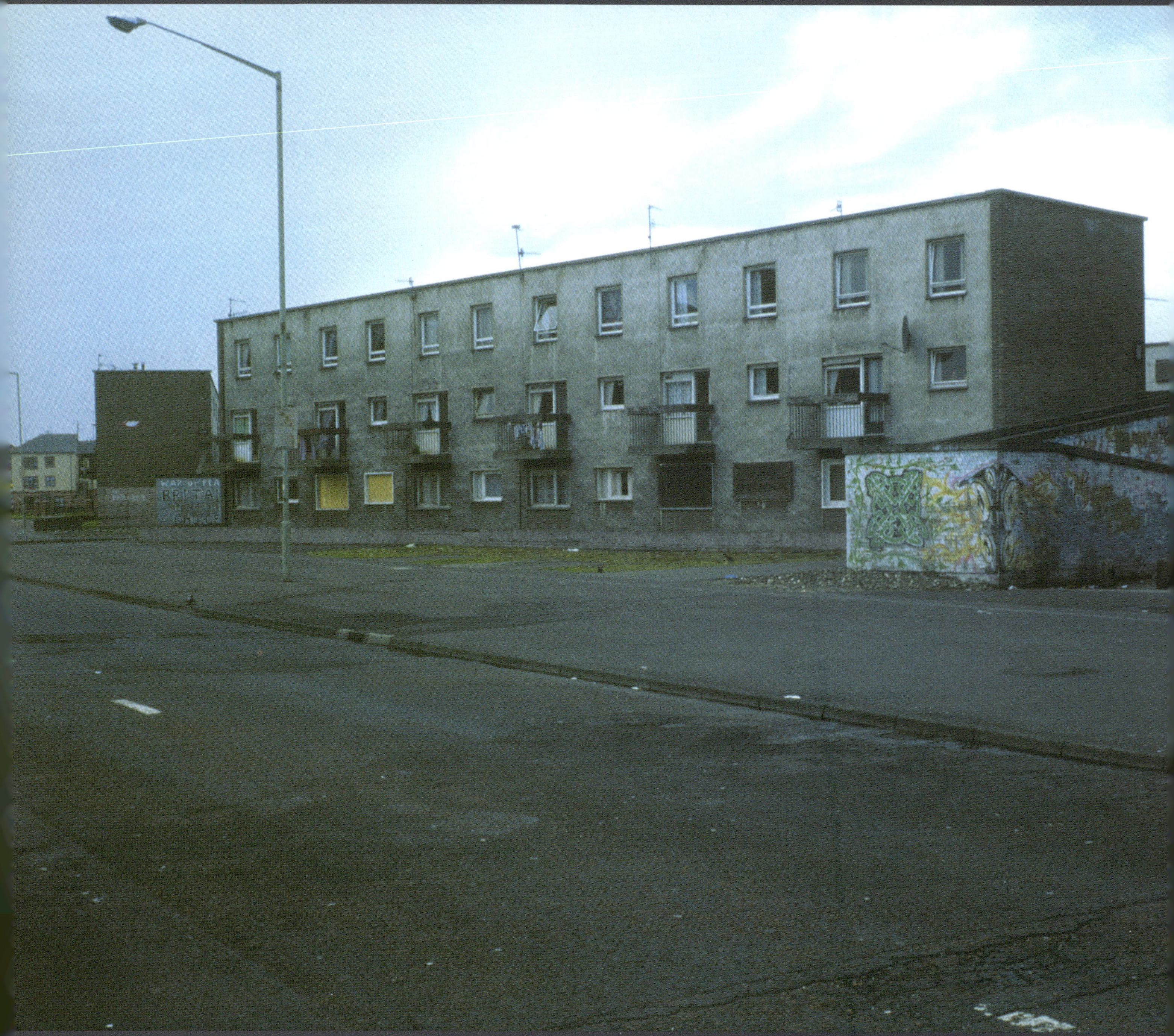

Derry, Northern Ireland (UK), June 20, 1999
#34 from the series *Voyages apocalyptiques*
C-Print, 46 x 58 cm

Another island: my holidays in Corsica, 40 slides
Photos: Jules Spinatsch, 1997
Orchard Gallery, Derry 1999

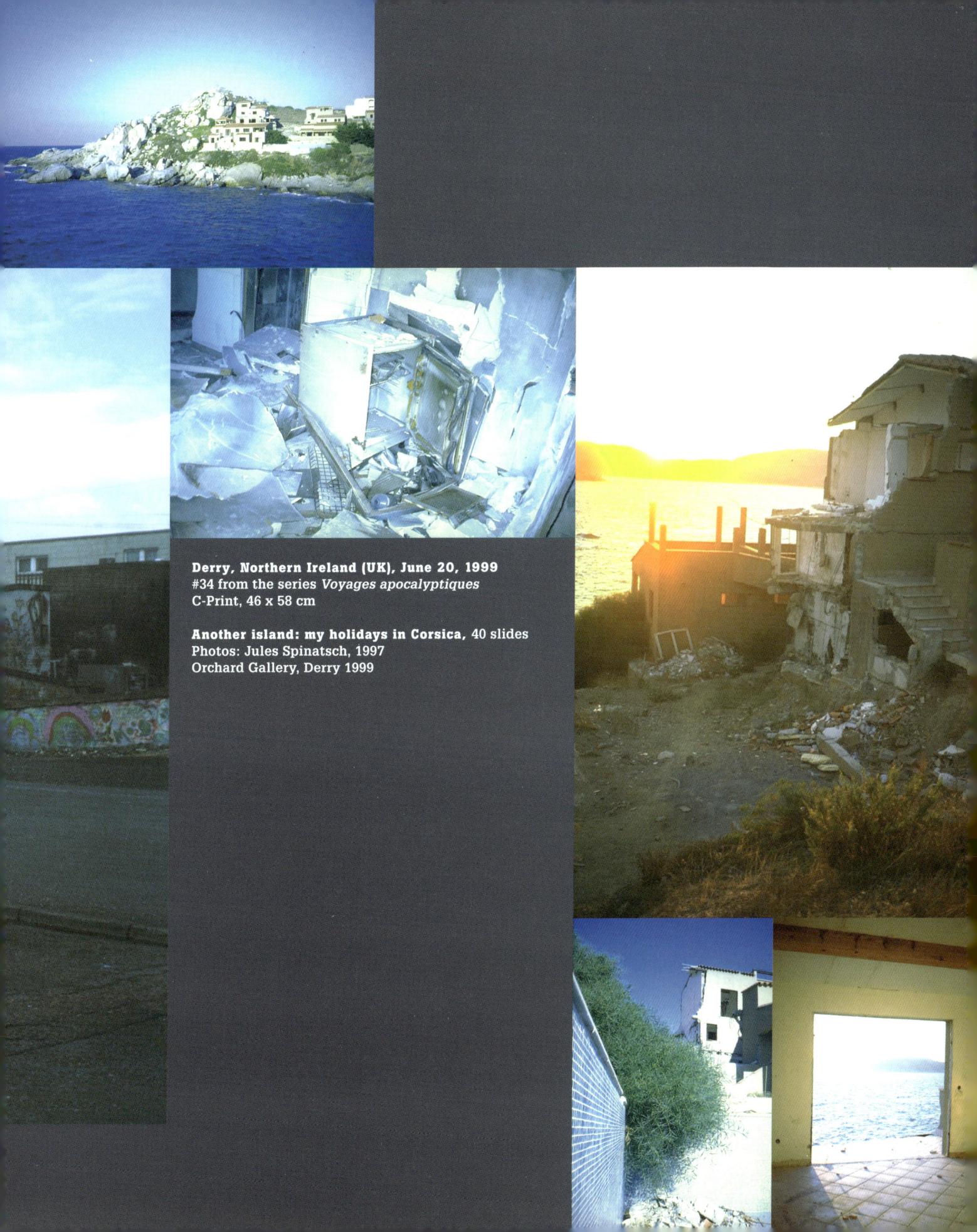

"It's right here where I'm gonna kill me a nigger"

Feel lucky, punk??!
Installation views *Cinéma, Cinéma,*
Van Abbe Museum Eindhoven, 1999
NB, Kunsthalle St. Gallen, 1998
2-channel video installation, 12 min 20
projection, sound, surveillance monitor
New York, 1997/98
Images from *Magnum Force,*
original version (left), and remake
(right, with Mikha Gaugh as cashier)

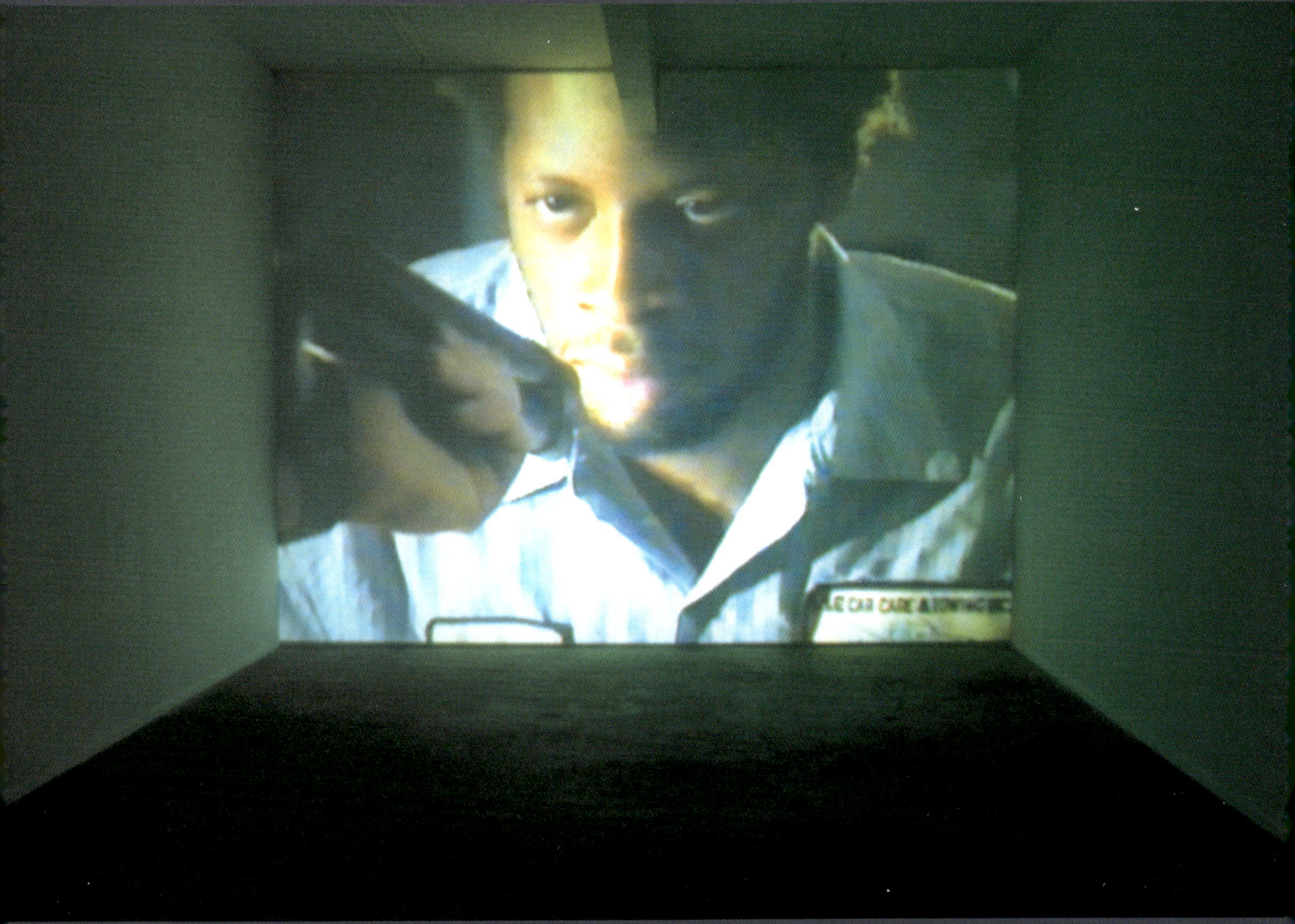

Good morning, ladies and gentlemen, this is a robbery! (detail)
C-print, 40 x 60 cm, still photography
by Heidrun Holzfeind
Scene from *Thelma & Louise* (remake)

Feel lucky, punk??!, video stills
Video, 12 min 20, 1998
(Remakes of *Pulp Fiction*, *Thelma & Louise*, *Magnum Force*, *Taxidriver*)

...then just execute him!!!
C-print, 40 x 60 cm, still photography
by Heidrun Holzfeind
Scene from *Pulp Fiction* (remake)

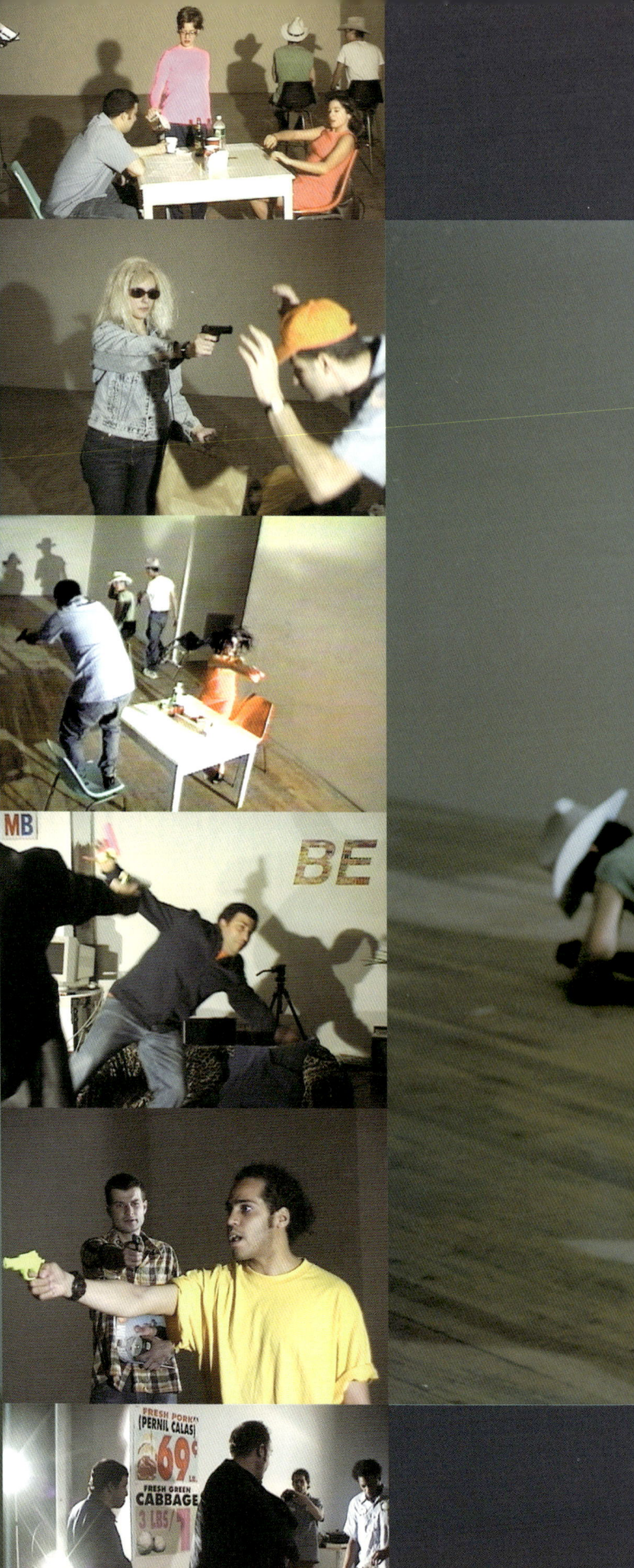

45

Serneus New York retour

Kulturhaus Rosengarten, Grüsch, 1998

Puzzled #2
Installation view Kulturhaus Rosengarten, Grüsch
Video projection, sound, 4 m³ puzzles, 3 monitors

Apocalypse now (projection)
Video VHS 20 min (found footage),
® usa – united swiss artist, 1994
In collaboration with Martin Frei
(Still image from *Sodom & Gomorrah*)

911 – emergency room (monitors)
Video DV 3 x 7 min, New York, 1997

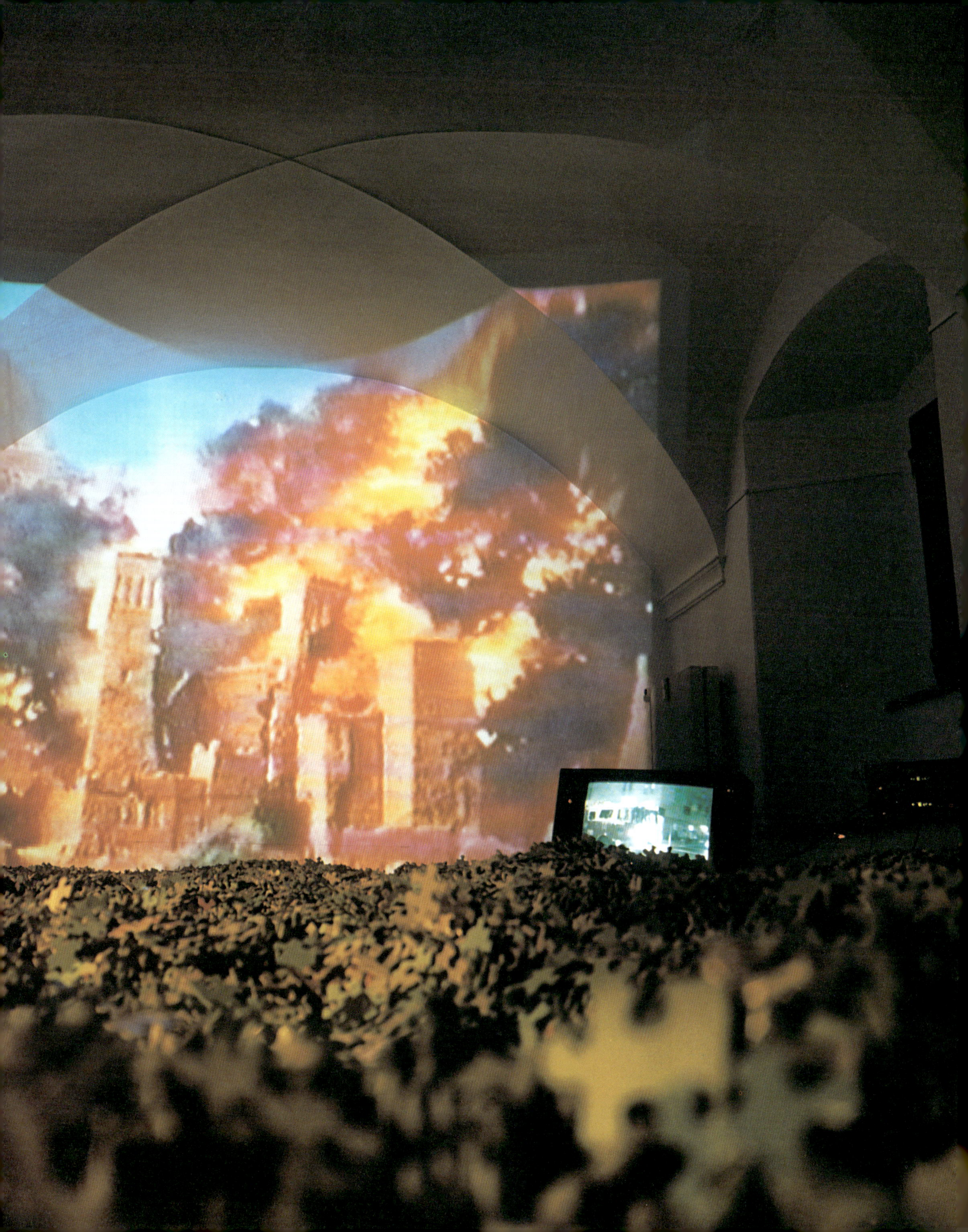

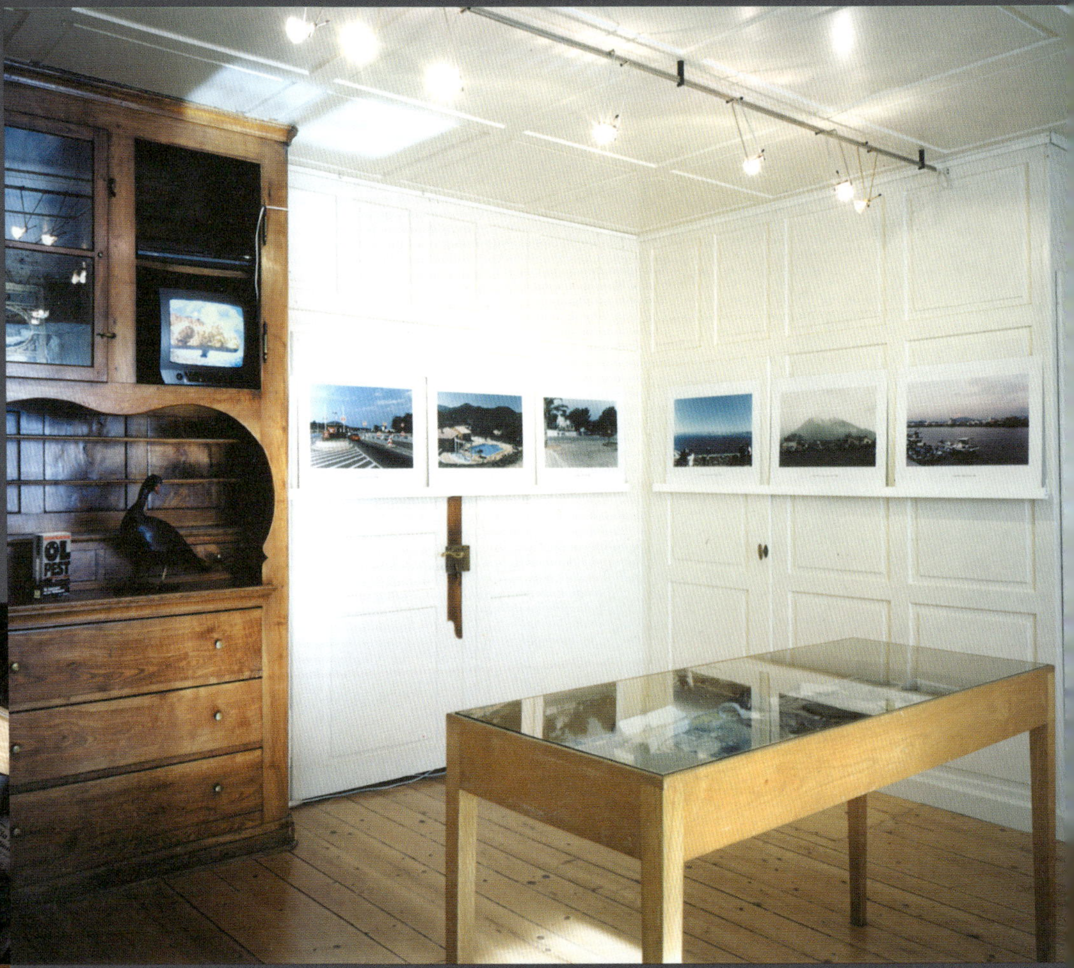
ÖL
PEST

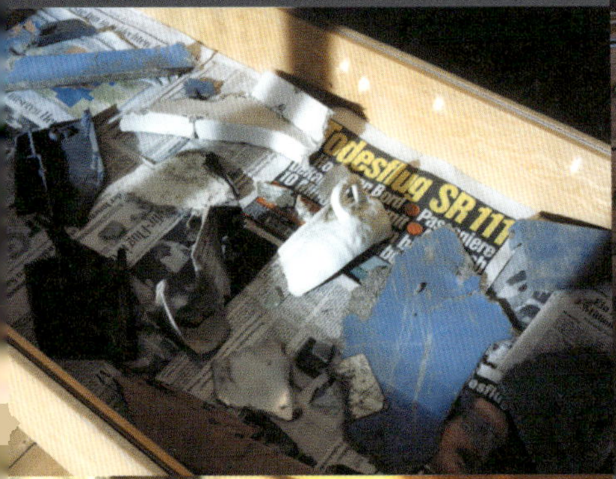
Todesflug SR 111

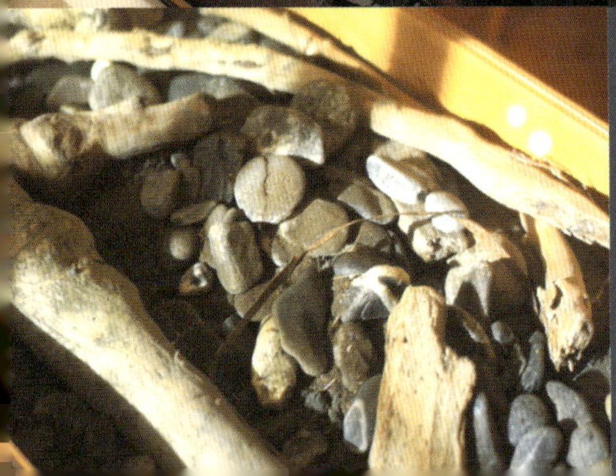

Serneus New York retour
Installation view
Kulturhaus Rosengarten, Grüsch
C-prints from the series
Voyages apocalyptiques, 1994–98
Video *Oel* (Oil), 13 min, 1998
Oelente (Oil Duck),
Oil on stuffed duck, 1995

Two displays
Debris from ICE 886,
newspaper clips about Swissair 111
Debris from the Grüsch flood, 1907

**Metropolis / SF 1908 /
Sodom & Gomorrah / Earthquake**
Blueprints 120 x 150 cm, 1995
(Stills from *Apocalypse now*)

Sodom & Gomorrah (Lea's last sight)
Blueprint 120 x 150 cm, 1995

Flood, Dalvazza, Prättigau, 1907
Acrylic paint jet on jigsaw puzzle,
4000 pcs, 96 x 136 cm

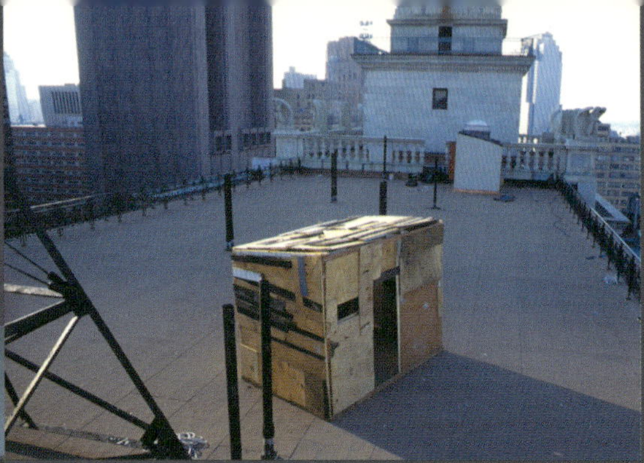

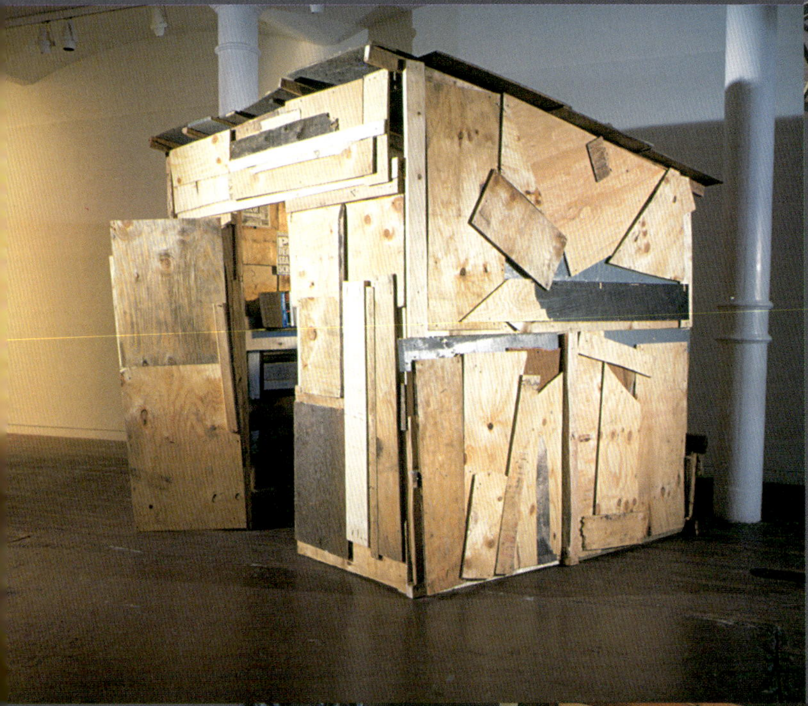

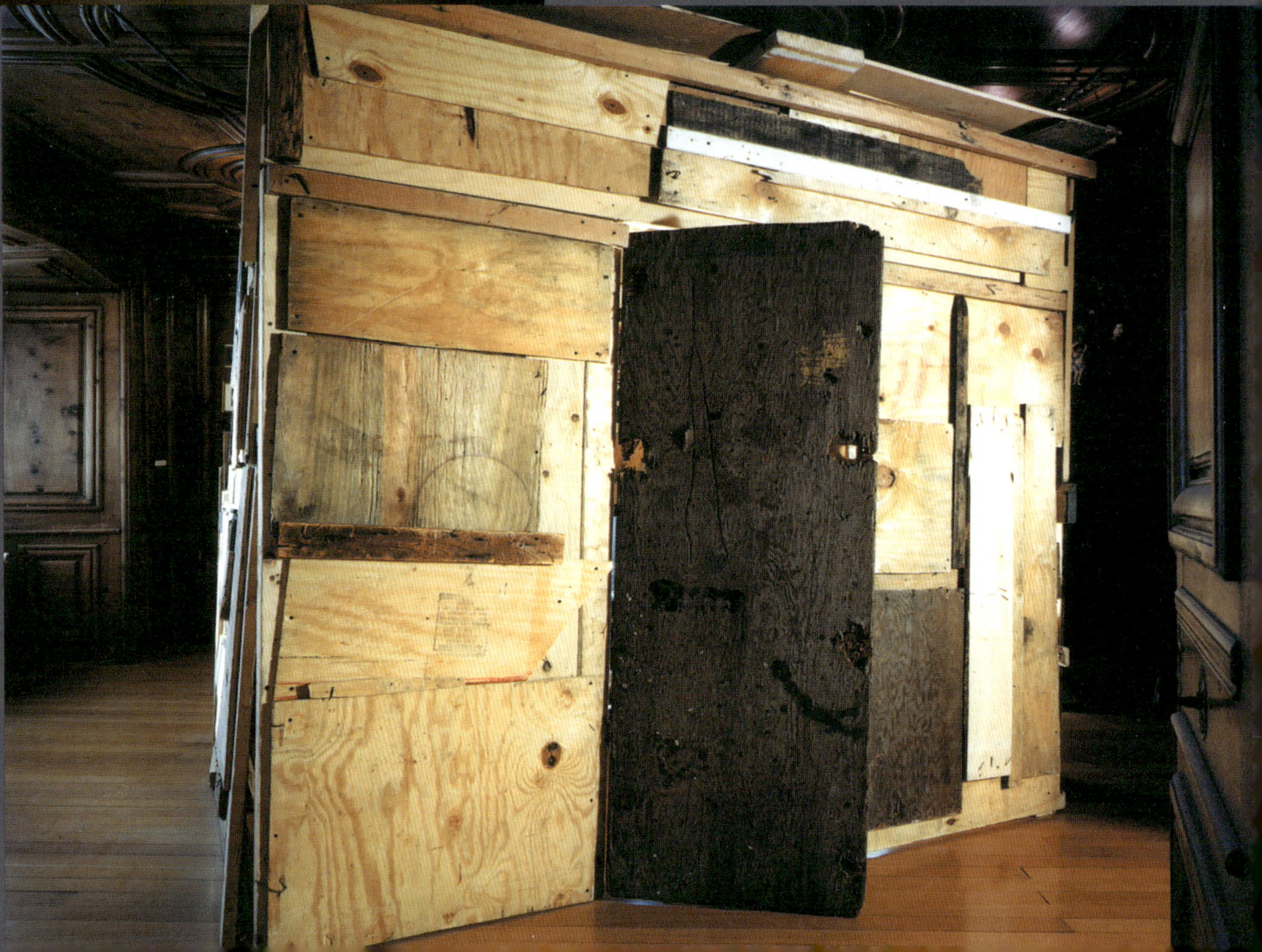

The shack
Wood, 4m x 3m x 2.5 m
P.S. 1, Institute for Contemporary Art,
Clocktower Roof, 1996

The shack
Disaster and recovery,
Swiss Institute, New York, 1996

The shack
Serneus New York retour,
Kulturhaus Rosengarten, Grüsch, 1998

The shack (interiors)
TV, tapeplayer, clips from magazines,
book covers, lamp, trophy, etc

The three days of darkness, video stills
Prophecies of the end of the world
Video, 90 min, 1997
(from *Ancient prophecies*)

The shack / 911 – emergency room
Installation view
NB, Kunsthalle St. Gallen, 1998

52

911 – emergency room
Installation view and video stills
NB, Kunsthalle St. Gallen, 1998
4 video projections on 4 walls,
quadrophonic sound, 7 min

Zur Lokalisierung der Endzeit
Daniel Binswanger

In gewisser Weise erinnern die Arbeiten Christoph Draegers an die unglaublichen Abenteuer des Soldaten Tyron Slothrope. Der Romanheld aus Pynchons *Gravity's Rainbow* gerät bekanntlich in die Mühlen undurchdringlicher Geheimdienstintrigen und verliert sich in den paranoischen Wirrnissen des europäischen Schlachtfeldes in den letzten Monaten des Zweiten Weltkrieges, weil er eine kleine physiologische Besonderheit aufweist: immer wenn die Nazis einen Raketenangriff auf London starten, kriegt Slothrope eine Erektion, und zwar genau an der Einschlagstelle und bevor das Desaster hereinbricht. Seine Überreiztheit führt Slothrope jedesmal dazu, erotische Abenteuer zu suchen, und anschließend markiert er Ort und Datum seiner einschlägigen Aktivitäten auf einem Stadtplan. Es ist dann nur eine Frage der Zeit, bis Statistiker des amerikanischen Geheimdienstes auf die geheimnisvolle Korrelation von Erektionen und Explosionen aufmerksam werden und Slothropes seltsame Sensibilität in den Dienst höherer Mächte genommen wird. Es bleibt Slothrope schließlich nur noch eine alptraumhafte Höllenfahrt ins Herz seiner eigenen Konditionierung. Er schlägt sich in die «Zone» durch, ins zusammenbrechende Nazireich, um die Abschußrampen seines eigenen Todestriebes zu finden.

Von einer ähnlich physischen Anziehung scheint Christoph Draeger besessen zu sein. Wo immer auf dem Globus eine Katastrophe geschieht, will Draeger sie registrieren. Es geht ihm dabei nicht darum, mit immer neuen Bildern des Grauens sich am Erhabenen die Zähne auszubeißen. Draeger läßt sich Zeit. In der Regel kommt er erst, wenn alles wieder aufgeräumt ist. Aber er arbeitet unbeirrbar an einer imaginären Kartographie des Desaströsen: der Ort wird besucht, ein Datum fixiert, das Desaster lokalisiert. Dies ist umso dringlicher als das Böse gleichsam staatenlos geworden ist: im Gegensatz zu den Verhältnissen des Jahres 1945 ist es nicht ohne weiteres in einer deutschen Zone zu verorten. Auch die Typologie des Desasters scheint reicher geworden zu sein. Draegers Obsession ist bemerkenswert polymorph. Erdbeben, Flugzeugabstürze, Amokläufe: alles wird fein säuberlich eingetragen. Die Frage ist nicht mehr: welchen Ursprung hat die Katastrophe? In welcher Zone findet sie statt? Die Frage lautet: welche Zone schafft die Katastrophe? Oder ganz einfach: wo ist die Zone? Das war lange Zeit keine Frage. In der guten alten Bundesrepublik wußte man, was die «Zone» ist. Es war die offiziöse Bezeichnung für das Territorium der DDR. Man gab damit zu verstehen, daß es sich um illegitim besetztes Gebiet handelte, ein Hoheitsgebiet ohne eigentliche Hoheit, in einem ebenso uneigentlichen und gespenstischen Raum. Die Zone war der Ort eines geschichtlich zu sühnenden Unrechts. Das Wort in dieser Bedeutung ist folglich mit dem Mau-

On the Localization of Apocalypse
Daniel Binswanger

In a certain way, the works of Christoph Draeger are reminiscent of the unbelievable adventure of the soldier Tyron Slothrope. The hero of Pynchon's novel *Gravity's Rainbow* is run through the mill of impenetrable secret-agent intrigues and loses himself in the paranoid chaos of the European killing fields in the last months of Second World War, due to a small physiological peculiarity: Whenever the Nazis initiate a bomb attack on London, Slothrope gets an erection at the exact location of the attack before disaster strikes. Slothrope's oversensitivity leads him to seek erotic adventures. He subsequently marks, with date and location, his pertinent activities on a city map. It is then just a question of time before the statisticians of the American secret service become aware of the mysterious correlation between erections and explosions, and Slothrope's strange sensitivities are used for higher purposes. All that remains for Slothrope is a nightmarish trip into the heart of his own conditioning. He enters the "zone" – into the emerging Nazi reich – to find the terminus of his death wish.

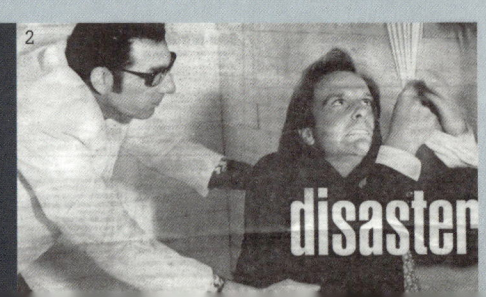

erfall aus dem deutschen Vokabular verschwunden. Im französischen tauchte dagegen anfangs der neunziger Jahre sein gespenstischer Erbe auf. Man begann in Paris häufiger von den *zonards* zu reden, die man auf den Straßen sieht, und man sah davon immer mehr. Der *zonard* ist das schattenhafte Erscheinungsbild all jener, die eigentlich nicht mehr erscheinen können, weil ihnen im sozialen Raum kein Platz zugestanden wird. Es sind jene Legionen von arbeitslosen Vorstadtjugendlichen, die weder Geld noch Perspektiven noch irgendeine Identität haben, und die in ihren Jogging-Hosen durch die Innenstädte geistern, ohne daß irgend jemand wüßte, woher sie kommen und wohin sie wieder verschwinden. Sie gehören eben in die Zone, Bewohner jener Nichtorte, die man heute Zonen nennt. Die soziale Desintegration hat die Zonen radikaler Illegitimität so nahe an uns herangetragen, daß wir von äußeren Feinden und dem Reich des Bösen nur noch träumen können. Die Zone ist das Desaster. Sie ist allgegenwärtig, d.h. sie ist nirgends. Sie bestimmt die sozialen Räume nach dem Kollaps der historischen Koordinaten-Systeme.

Draegers Bedürfnis nach einer neuen Geographie der Katastrophen reagiert auch auf die Hypertrophie des Desaströsen, seit die Welt aus der Hypnose durch die Drohung der atomaren Apokalypse erwacht ist. Die Katastrophe liegt weder vor noch hinter uns, aber sie geschieht. Draegers Gemächlichkeit ist das Symptom jenes unentrinnbaren Zuspätkommens, das man als *posthistoire* zu denken versucht hat. Was bedeutet es aber, in einer «Spätzeit» zu leben, in einer seltsam desartikulierten Zeit, die nach der Formel, die Hamlet auf die Schwelle der Neuzeit geschrieben hat («the time is out of joints»), ganz einfach aus den Fugen geraten ist?

3

Christoph Draeger seems to be obsessed with a similar physical attraction. Wherever on the globe a catastrophe occurs, Draeger wants to record it. His work has nothing to do with finding the sublime in the endless flood of new images of darkness. Draeger takes his time. He generally arrives after the debris is already cleared, but he works unerringly on an imaginary cartography of disaster: The place is visited, the date fixed, the disaster located. This process is ever more penetrating as evil loses its nationality; in contrast to conditions in 1945, localizing disasters extends far beyond German soil. Even the typology of the disasters seems to have become richer. Draeger's obsession is noticeably polymorphous. Earthquakes, airplane crashes, riots – everything is finely, cleanly registered. The question is no longer one of the origins of the catastrophe, or where it takes place. It is a question of which zone the catastrophe creates; or simply, where is the zone? This was, for a long time, not a relevant question. In the good old Federal Republic of Germany, one knew what the "zone" was; it was the designation for the territory of the GDR. One understood that the zone had to do with an illegitimately occupied area, a kingdom without an actual monarch in an equally ingenuine and ghostlike area. The zone was the location of an historical misdeed, one which required atonement. This meaning of the word "zone" has disappeared from the German vocabulary with the fall of the Berlin Wall. In France, however, a strange inheritance emerged at the beginning of the nineties. Parisians began to speak more and more frequently of the *zonard* one would see on the street, and one saw more and more of them. The *zonard* is the shadowy image of those who actually are invisible because there is no room made for them in the social structure. They consist of legions of unemployed suburban youths possessing neither money nor future nor any kind of identity; who traipse through the inner cities in their jogging pants without anyone knowing where they came from and to whence they will disappear. They belong in the zone, inhabitants of the no-man's-land that one now calls the zone. The social disintegration has brought the zones' radical illegitimacy so near that we can only dream of enemies and the realm of evil. The zone is the disaster. It is all-encompassing, which means it is nowhere. It determines social areas, after the collapse of the historical system of coordinates. Draeger's need for a new geography of catastrophes reacts to the hypertrophy of the disastrous, since the world has been awakened from its hypnosis through the atomic apocalypse. Catastrophe lies neither behind us nor before us, but simply occurs. Draeger's ease is a symptom of inescapable tardiness that one attempts to designate as *posthistoire.* But what does it mean to live in a "post" time, a time taking after the formula that Hamlet wrote of on the brink of the new age ("the time is out of joints") – simply out of whack?

MAURICE BLANCHOT

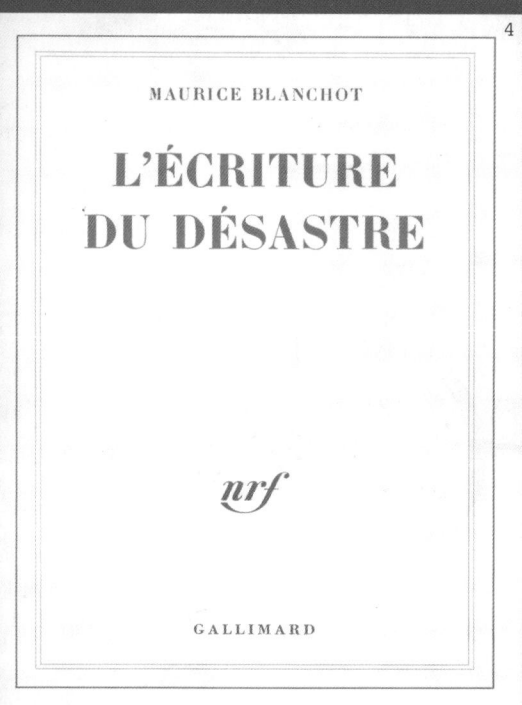

L'ÉCRITURE
DU DÉSASTRE

nrf

GALLIMARD

Nothing would be further from the truth than to believe that Draeger's art will make us wise, that everything is simply over anyway; that we can now fall into frivolity. He plays virtuously with a silly aesthetic, however, in *Feel lucky punk??!*, but the majority of his issues are slightly more deceptive. Our latecomer's decadence cannot make it easy for us (decadence is always a very puzzling and/or an eternally boring condition). It belongs to the classic scheme of historical philosophy, one that can follow neither from tragedy nor comedy. The motif is already determined for the Hegelian aesthetic, which declares modern art dead and will only offer it a niche in the delicate humor of a Jean-Paul. With Marx, the same recognition becomes an angry outrage: The tragedies of the story repeat themselves as a farce. It is valid, then, for a tragedy to create a radical end. With Alexandre Kojève,

Nichts wäre verfehlter, als zu glauben, daß Draegers Kunst uns weismachen will, es sei nun eben alles vorbei und wir könnten in die Frivolität abgleiten. Zwar spielt er in seinem *Feel lucky punk??!* virtuos mit einer Ästhetik des Rumalberns, aber die Dinge sind durchaus etwas hinterhältiger. Einfach darf es sich unsere Spätlings-Dekadenz nicht machen (Dekadenz ist immer ein äußerst verzwickter oder aber unendlich langweiliger Zustand). Es gehört zum klassischen Schema der Geschichtsphilosophie, daß auf die Tragödie nur noch die Komödie folgen kann. Das Motiv ist bereits bestimmend für die Ästhetik von Hegel, der die moderne Kunst für tot erklärt und ihr nur noch eine Nische im feinsinnigen Humor eines Jean Paul zugestehen will. Bei Marx wird dieselbe Erkenntnis zu einem zornigen Aufschrei: die Tragödien der Geschichte wiederholen sich als Farce. Es gilt also der originator of the term *posthistoire*, we find ourselves in a Stalinist Biedermeier. The substance of history is ripped open, only formal games remain. Because history has ended, we live after its completion, nothing more can happen. The world remains as a perfect and totally integrated functional unity. The embodiment of this condition, for Kojève, was father Stalin. Kojève transfigured the Cold War into a global vacation paradise, which now only follows when the neo-liberal hymns of triumphing globalization sing to the same melody. Stalin has landed in the wax museum of historical monsters, but Doctor Strangelove's children now celebrate the achievement and perfection of *posthistoire:* The future is reduced to changes in course. The capitalistic version of this totalitarian "everything is over" credo has seamlessly survived the change in the times.

Draeger's work does not want to fit into this long tradition of historical philosophy. He is, like all of us, confronted with the same problems, but things appear for him in a different light. This is apparent in Draeger's

der Tragik ein radikales Ende zu machen. Mit Alexandre Kojève, dem Erfinder des Begriffs des *posthistoire*, sind wir in einem stalinistischen Biedermeier angelangt: die Substanz der Geschichte ist aufgezehrt, es bleiben uns nur noch formelle Spielereien. Weil die Geschichte an ihr Ende kam, leben wir nach der Vollendung: nichts kann mehr geschehen, die Welt ist nur noch ein perfekter und total integrierter Funktionszusammenhang. Die Verkörperung dieses Zustands war für Kojève Väterchen Stalin. Kojève verklärte den kalten Krieg zum globalen Urlaubsparadies, und es ist nur folgerichtig, wenn heute die neoliberalen Hymnen der triumphierenden Globalisierung genau dieselbe Melodie anstimmen. Stalin ist ins Wachsfigurenkabinett der historischen Monster abgewandert, aber Doctor Strangeloves Kinder zelebrieren nun auf ihre Weise die Vollendung des *posthistoire:* die Zukunft reconfrontation with Japan. Kojève sees in Japan the perfect model of *posthistoire*. The absolute dead seriousness with which life, up to its very last predetermined rituals, is respected in the land of the rising sun – where everything is important, because nothing makes sense anymore. Draeger's works focusing on the Japanese earthquakes shift this accent. On the one hand, he is fascinated by the perfect simulation of the event. Catastrophes are moments in which the experience of reality is stronger than at other times. But the Japanese, through their constant preventative simulation of apocalypse, seem to want to sleekly remove its appearance. The perfect simulation seems to exactly follow the desubstantialization that forms the core of Kojève's perfection thesis. On the other hand, other moments exist in Draeger's videos. With a very precise view, he registers the absurd in these events – an absurdity that does not unwrap the overwhelming sensory emptiness of the artificial world, but rather brings to light the odd reality of its all-too-human helplessness. In a sequence of videos shot in Japan, Draeger films a traffic policeman who appears to be

duziert sich auf Kursschwankungen. Mühelos hat die kapitalistische Version dieses totalitären «Alles ist vorbei» den Zeitenwechsel überstanden.

In diese lange Tradition der Geschichtsphilosophie will Draegers Arbeit nicht hineinpassen. Er ist – wie wir alle – mit derselben Problematik konfrontiert, aber die Dinge erscheinen in einem anderen Licht. Ersichtlich wird dies in Draegers Auseinandersetzung mit Japan. Kojève erblickt in Japan das perfekte Modell des *posthistoire*. Der absolute Todernst, mit dem im Land der aufgehenden Sonne die Formen der das Leben bis ins letzte bestimmenden Rituale respektiert werden, scheint jenen Zustand zu realisieren, in dem alles wichtig ist, weil nichts mehr Sinn macht. Draegers Arbeiten über den Katastrophenarchipel Japan verschieben den Akzent. Zum einen ist er fasziniert von der perfekten Simulation der Ereignisse. Katastrophen sind Augenblicke, in denen die Erfahrung der Realität stärker ist denn je, aber in Japan scheint man durch das ständige präventive Simulieren der Apokalypse schlicht ihr Eintreten abschaffen zu wollen. Die perfekte Simulation scheint genau die Entsubstantialisierung zu verfolgen, die den Kern von Kojèves Vollendungsthese bildet. Andererseits aber zeigt sich in Draegers Videos noch ein anderes Moment. Mit sehr präzisem Blick registriert er das Absurde dieser ganzen Veranstaltungen – eine Absurdität, die nicht die gewaltsame Sinnleere der künstlichen Welten enthüllt, sondern das seltsam Wirkliche ihrer allzumenschlichen Unbeholfenheit zum Vorschein bringt. In einer langen Sequenz des Japanvideos filmt Draeger einen Verkehrspolizisten, der mitten auf einer Straßenkreuzung einen streng choreographierten Tempeltanz aufzuführen scheint. Man lacht, und zugleich hat dieser Blick auf die Japan Inc. etwas Subversives. So sehr Draeger auch inhaltlich fixiert ist auf Katastrophen, formell nähren sich seine Arbeiten eher von einer Poesie der Panne. Die tönerne Idenmise of rebuilding and apocalypse. Apocalypse is, in its literal meaning, the moment of exposure of truth, the point of fleeing history, which in its deepest sense always remains the history of recovery. It is the absolutely ambivalent moment of absolute reality. The reporting of catastrophes follows the same pattern: Only he who shows how horrid reality can be can have something substantial to say about what it really is. The promise of recovery attempts to make this ambivalence bearable. It anticipates the end. Therefore, the perfection of history drives us further into the simulation of apocalypse. The fascination for the virtual worlds that permeate our present lives takes its sustenance as much from the will to create an artificial paradise as from the desire to sacrifice the real world. The dissolution of being that exists in utopian worlds is bound to the destruction of the real world, and destruction becomes the reference point of the real. Everything that is perfect is of strange ambivalence, and every absolute promise of happiness contains a horrifying threat. Even the new Eden of cyberspace demands the propitiatory tität des *posthistoire* entlarvt sich als ideologisches Konstrukt, wenn sie vor dem fein registrierenden Blick der Videokamera immer wieder ins Strauchen gerät.

Man wird deshalb nicht sagen können, daß Draeger Katastrophen simuliert. Simulation und Katastrophe stehen im selben Verhältnis wie Heilsversprechen und Apokalypse. Die Apokalypse ist, im eigentlichen Wortsinn, der Augenblick der Enthüllung der Wahrheit, der Fluchtpunkt der Geschichte, die in ihrem vollen Sinne immer Heilsgeschichte bleibt. Sie ist der absolut ambivalente Moment der absoluten Realität. Die Katastrophenmeldung verfährt nach demselben Muster: nur wer zeigt, wie schlimm es in der Wirklichkeit kommen kann, scheint etwas Wesentliches zu sagen darüber, was Wirklichkeit überhaupt ist. Das Heilsversprechen versucht diese Ambivalenz erträgbar zu machen: es antizipiert das Ende, entschärft seine Drohung und beschwört sein Eintreffen. Der Traum von der Vollendung der Geschichte treibt uns deshalb immer weiter in die Simulation der Apokalypse. Die Faszination für die virtuellen Welten,

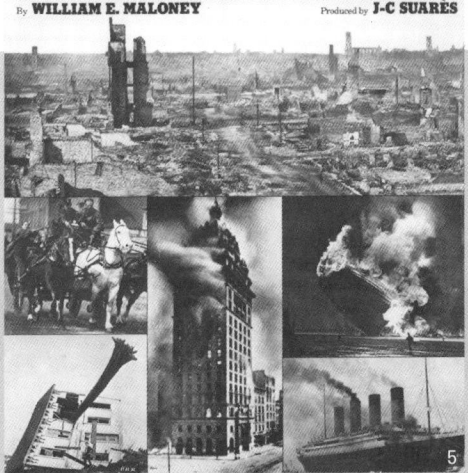

executing a strictly choreographed temple dance in the middle of an intersection. One laughs, and this look at Japan, Inc. has something subversive. As much as Draeger fixates on catastrophes in his content, the form of his works approaches more of a poetry of disaster. The earthen identity of *posthistoire* exposes itself as an ideological construct when it trips over itself in front of the scrupulous lens of the video camera.

One cannot say that Draeger simulates catastrophes. Simulation and catastrophe stand in the same relationship to the pro-

die heute unser Leben überziehen, lebt genauso von dem Willen, künstliche Paradiese zu erzeugen, wie von dem Wunsch, die wirkliche Welt zu opfern. Die Auflösung des Seins in paradiesische, mögliche Welten ist gebunden an die Vernichtung der wirklichen Welt, weil dann die Vernichtung selbst zum Bezugspunkt des Realen wird. Alles Perfekte ist von unheimlicher Ambivalenz, und jedes absolute Glücksversprechen beinhaltet eine entsetzliche Drohung. Auch das neue Eden des Cyberspace verlangt nach dem sühnenden Opfer der alten Welt: es erstrebt die Vollendung durch Abschaffung, die Sühne durch den Holocaust, dem sich durch die neuen Horizonte totaler technischer Machbarkeit schwindelerregende Horizonte eröffnen. Bei Draeger scheinen neue Technologien nicht auf virtuelle Perfektion abzuzielen, sondern sie bilden die Werkzeuge, mit denen er Gebilde montiert, die die Simulation zerstören.

Die Verknüpfung von Katastrophe und Heilsgeschichte, die zum Kern aller Geschichtsphilosophie gehört und in Kojèves *posthistoire* ebenso wie in der entsprechenden Variante der Postmoderne eine mächtige Renaissance erlebt, ist auch heute noch dominierend. Sie gehört zum scheinbar unausrottbaren teleologischen Orientierungsbedürfnis einer Zivilsation, der zweitausend Jahre Christentum in den Knochen stecken. Im zwanzigsten Jahrhundert hat aber auch insofern ein Umbruch stattgefunden, als wir es mit einer Apokalypse zu tun kriegten, die an heilsgeschichtlich nicht mehr zu bewältigende Unheimlichkeiten rührt. Angst hat in einer Weise Einzug gehalten, die als Schauder vor dem Heiligen nicht mehr zu verstehen ist. Kierkegaard hat den Begriff der Angst als den unheilbaren Riß im hegelschen System inszeniert, Heidegger hat versucht, in der Erfahrung der Angst den existentiellen Zugang zur Eigentlichkeit zu gründen, und Niklas Luhmann brachte diese grundlegende Dimension der Angst einmal auf folgende lapidare Formel: wenn moderne Gesellschaften überhaupt ein a priori haben, so ist es die Angst. Es handelt sich nicht mehr um eine prospektive Beschwörung absoluter Realität, sondern um eine konstitutive Unsicherheit. Niemand hat diese neue, alles begründende und alles annulierende Qualität des Desaströsen obsessiver umkreist als Maurice Blanchot.

Was ist nach Maurice Blanchot ein Desaster? In bester mystischer Tradition könnte man sagen: es ist jenes nichts, jene Vernichtung, die alles ermöglicht, der Horizont allen Denkens, der selber nicht zu denken ist. In immer neuen Wendungen wird der Ursprung umkreist. Interessant sind dabei weniger die paradoxen Strukturen, die immer zum Tragen kommen, wenn unhintergängliche Denkdimensionen ergründet werden, sondern die Tatsache, daß der Begriff des Desasters jene Ursprünglichkeit in besonderer Ungreifbarkeit zu artikulieren erlaubt. Das Desaster ist die Ungreifbarkeit selber. Zunächst führt dies zu einer seltsamen Entzeitlichung. Zwar gehört das

sacrifice of the old world. It strives for perfection through removal and destruction, atonement through this Holocaust, a Holocaust that opens dizzying horizons through the new worlds of complete technological capabilities. With Draeger, new technologies seem not to aim for virtual perfection, but, rather, build the tools with which he mounts the creations that destroy simulation.

The connection between catastrophe and the promise of recovery (existing at the core of all historical philosophy, and experiencing a powerful renaissance in Kojève's *posthistoire* as well as in the corresponding variations of postmodern theory) is still predominant today. It belongs to the apparently irrevocable teleological need for orientation of any civilization with two thousand years of Christianity imbedded in its marrow. In the twentieth century, however, a sort of breakthrough has occurred, as we were forced to confront an apocalypse that touched upon insurmountable atrocities. In a way, fear made its entrance as shuddering before the holy made its exit. Kierkegaard exposed the idea of fear as the irreparable tear in the Hegelian system. Heidegger attempted to establish an existential doorway to reality through the experience of fear, and Niklas Luhmann brought the fundamental dimension of fear to the following concise formula: If modern society has an a priori at all, it is fear. It is

après-coup zum Grundgestus von Blanchots denken, das Desaster ist uns immer schon vorausgegangen, aber man darf dieses *nachher* nicht eigentlich zeitlich verstehen. Blanchot sagt klar, daß das Desaster weder räumlich noch zeitlich zu verstehen ist. Raum und Zeit werden erst ermöglicht durch die Öffnung, die das Desaster spendet. Das Desaster wird zur sakralen Gabe überhaupt, das das Sein stiftet, und zugleich ist es jene Grundbewegung, die alles annulliert. Es geht nicht mehr um die moralische Frage von Gut und Böse oder von Glück und Unglück, sondern der Begriff wird ontologisch gewendet und bezeichnet jenes *clair-obscur*, indem die Ursprünge verdämmern. Es gibt bei Blanchot nichts von der hitzigen Überstürztheit des Hereinbrechens eines Ereignisses, sondern das Pathos des Desasters strahlt eine seltsame Kühle aus. Das Desaster geht uns nichts an, es ist, was uns in eine unheilbare Indifferenz stößt. Es trifft uns nie, und das ist unsere einzige und unausweichliche Betroffenheit. Anderswo hat Blanchot dies unter dem Begriff der Unpersönlichkeit des Seins thematisiert: wir können unser Sein nicht bewohnen, denn es ist eine anonyme Wüste. Das Desaster artikuliert nicht mehr die ambivalente Realität des absoluten Bezugspunkts, sondern es die alles durchsetzende Beziehungslosigkeit. Blanchot bringt mit seinen ontologischen Reflexionen sicherlich eine Grundstimmung der Epoche auf den Begriff. Bei Heidegger hat der Angstbegriff noch einen heroischen Akzent. Wer sich ganz auf sie einläßt und «in seinen eigenen Tod vorläuft» (die prospektive, zeitliche Dimension, die zum heilsgeschichtlichen Erbe gehört, bleibt), der wird zum «Helden» seiner eigenen Existenz. Blanchots unterkühltes und staubtrockenes Pathos ist wie ein Schleier von alles durchdringenden Giftpartikeln, der sich über die Welt gelegt hat. Es scheint hier die seltsame Melancholie des Informationszeitalters auf: nur Desaster sind noch Geschehnisse, und das bedeutet, daß nichts mehr geschieht.

Es darf deshalb nicht wundern, daß Jean Baudrillard sehr verwandte Vorstellungen zur Grundlage seiner Zeitgeistdiagnostik macht. Was Blanchot mit dem Desaster bezeichnet, nennt Baudrillard schlicht das Böse. Der scheinbare semantische Umschwung ins Moralische dient allerdings nur der provokativen Zuspitzung: das Böse bezeichnet hier die strukturelle Grundgegebenheit des heutigen Daseins. Als solches ist es transparent geworden. Es hat sein Geheimnis, seinen Schauer und seine Verführung verloren. Es bezeichnet nicht mehr jenen Bereich der Transgression, in dem aus dem Ordnungszusammenhang der Welt ausgebrochen wird, jenen Zustand der Gnade, indem Verbrechen manchmal revolutionär sein können. Das Verbrechen, die Revolution und die Befreiung haben ausgespielt, denn alles und jeder ist «befreit» im triumphierenden Liberalismus (immerhin

no longer a question of prospective summoning of absolute reality, but rather one of established insecurity. No one examines this new, all-encompassing and all-annulling quality of the disastrous more obsessively than Maurice Blanchot.

What is disaster, according to Maurice Blanchot? In the best mystical tradition one could say it is about nothing, about destruction that makes everything possible; the horizon of thinking that is in itself incomprehensible. Its origin is contemplated in constantly new ways. What is interesting is less the paradoxical structures that always come to bear when dimensions of thought are examined, than the fact that the concept of disaster defies articulating any origin. Disaster is intangibility itself. And this leads to a strange timelessness. While the *aprés-coup* belongs to the foundation of Blanchot's thought, disaster has always preceded us. But one cannot temporally comprehend the "after". Blanchot states clearly that disaster can be understood neither temporally nor spatially. Time and space are only made possible through the opening that disaster creates. Disaster becomes a sacral gift, a gift that donates existence, but is at the same time the founding movement that annuls everything. It is no longer the moral question of good or evil, happiness or unhappiness. The concept is, rather, ontologically turned and defines every *clair-obscur* that illuminates its origins. With Blanchot, it is not the heated rush of an event's breakout, but the pathos of disaster that emits a strange coolness. Disaster has nothing to do with us, it is what pushes us into an irrevocable indifference. It never meets us, which is our sole sensitivity to it. Blanchot thematized this under the concept of impersonality of being. We cannot inhabit our being, as it is an anonymous wasteland. Disaster no longer articulates the ambivalent reality of the absolute reference point, but rather the encompassing lack of reference. With his ontological reflection, Blanchot defines the foundational zeitgeist of an epoch. Heidegger's definition of fear still has an heroic accent. He who lets himself completely go and "runs into his own death" (the prospective, temporal dimension belonging to the inheritance of recovery remains) becomes a "hero" of his own existence. Blanchot's cool and dry pathos is like a veil protecting us from the penetrating poisonous particles that have settled over the world. It illuminates here the odd melancholy of the information age: Disasters are now the only genuine occurrences, meaning that nothing anymore occurs.

It is not surprising that Jean Baudrillard makes very similar ideas the foundation of his diagnosis of the *zeitgeist*. What Blanchot describes as disaster, Baudrillard calls

hält Baudrillard doch noch an der Utopie des perfekten Verbrechens fest). Man kann an die bestehende Ordnung nicht durchbrechen, weil ihre Überschreitung ein Teil der Ordnung ist: das ist die berühmte These vom Tod der Kritik. Allerdings werden dadurch die Ordnungsprinzipien selber unüberblickbar. Sie sind zwar vollkommen transparent, da ihnen die Aura der Autorität fehlt, aber sie werden diffus. Baudrillard spricht deshalb von dem fraktalen Gesetz der Werte, die uns heute bestimmen. Eine Negation ist nur eine Iterationsschleife, die das Mandelbrot-Bäumchen noch etwas bunter macht, das ganze Umfeld aber wird chaotischer. Das Böse ist die Konfusion: es schlägt nicht mehr zu, es wuchert. Der Horizont wurde verschluckt vom absoluten Durchblick. Der Katastrophenbericht, der Draegers Arbeit inspiriert, wird dadurch gleich in zweifacher Hinsicht zum Emblem der Zeit. Einerseits nährt er die Hypertrophie der chaotischen Ordnung. Das Flimmern der Bildschirme ringt der transparenten Welt das Flimmern des Realen ab. Und andererseits bedient er unsere Nostalgie für moralische Orientierung: voller Er-

leichterung stellen wir fest, daß die Welt immer noch böse ist. Draeger allerdings nimmt ein irritierende Umkehrung vor: die Katastrophen werden selbst beliebig, und zu sehen gibt es eigentlich nichts.

Wir versuchten den konzeptuellen Hintergrund zu zeichnen, mit dem Draegers Arbeiten zweifellos spielen. Dennoch scheint es, daß seine Arbeiten in eine andere Richtung drängen. Das Desaster besetzt bei Draeger bestimmt nicht die Stelle der geschichtlichen Endzeit, aber auch Blanchots Ontologisierung oder Baudrillards Transparenz-These scheinen zur Konzeptualisierung seiner Werke nur bis an einen gewissen Punkt geeignet zu sein. Worum es Draeger darüber hinaus zu gehen scheint, ist eine durch all diese Strukturen hindurchgreifende Konkretheit. Seine Nüchternheit ist niemals melancholisch oder erhaben. Sie registriert und zählt auf: es gibt jenseits der Apokalypse noch ein Konkretes, das zum Erscheinen gebracht werden kann. Am frappierendsten scheint dabei der Zug zur Verräumlichung, wobei seine Umsetzung des Show-Downs aus Sergio Leo-

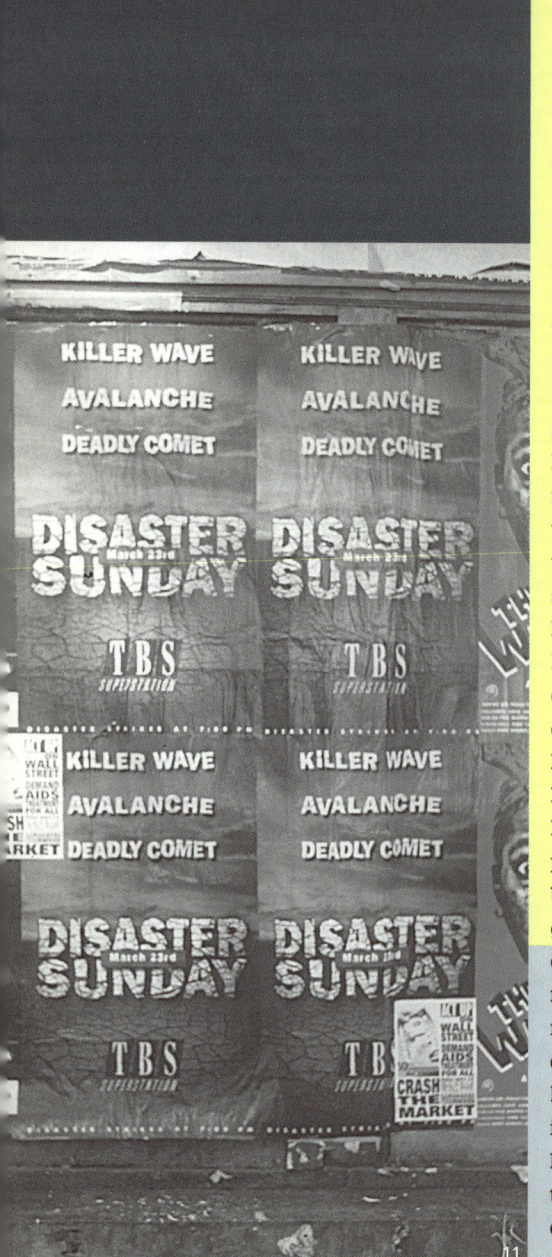

evil. The semantic swing to the moral makes a provocative point: Here, evil defines the structural foundation of our modern existence. It has become transparent. It has lost its secret, its thrill and seduction. It no longer defines the areas of transgression in which the structure of order in the world is broken; the state of grace in which crimes could be revolutionary. Crimes, revolutions, freedoms have been achieved, since, in the triumph of liberalism, everything and everyone is "freed" (although Baudrillard still clings to the utopia of the perfect crime). One cannot break through the existing order because its transgression is a part of the order – the famous thesis of the death of the critic. With this thesis, however, principles of order become unoverseeable. They are fully transparent because the aura of authority is missing; they become diffused. Baudrillard speaks, for this reason, of the fractal law of values defining us today. A negation is only a veil of iteration that makes the Mandelbrot sets a little more colorful while the rest of the environment becomes more chaotic. Evil is confusion. It hits us harder and harder, it proliferates. The horizon is swallowed by the absolute view. The reports of catastrophes that inspire Draeger's work become immediately a twofold emblem of our times. On the one hand, hypertrophy nourishes chaotic order. The flickering screens wring out the transparent, flickering real world. On the other hand, this hypertrophy serves our yearning for moral orientation. Relieved, we realize that the world is still evil. Draeger, however, takes on an irritating reversal: The catastrophes become life in themselves, and there's nothing to see.

We have attempted to draw up the conceptual background with which Draeger's work doubtless plays. It seems to us, however, that his works lean in another direction.

For Draeger, disaster does not occupy a historical terminus. And Blanchot's ontologization or Baudrillard's theory of transparence seem to conceptualize his work only to a certain point. It seems that Draeger's direction is to establish a basic solidity that transcends these structures. His sobriety is never melancholy or elevated; it registers and tabulates. There is, beyond the apocalypse, something concrete that can be brought to light. The most chilling seems to be the drive to expose the dimensions of disaster—his portrayal of the showdown from Sergio Leone's *Once Upon A Time in the West* can be thought of as exemplary. The film sequence is retranslated into its spatial dimension. The linear tension is so contorted that spaces emerge in which images of remembrance that hang over the scene can be localized. Draeger achieves a similar effect through the parallel montages of scenes from *Dirty Harry* or the spatial production of his videos, which appear to attribute locations to the images of disaster. Because it transcends boundaries, we cannot truly visualize disaster. We can neither expect not commemorate it because

nes *Spiel mir das Lied vom Tod* als exemplarisch gelten kann. Die Filmsequenz wird in ihr räumliches Dispositiv zurück-übersetzt. Der lineare Spannungseffekt wird so umgewandelt, daß sich Räume ergeben, in denen auch die Erinnerungsbilder, die über der Szene hängen, verortet werden können. Einen ähnlichen Effekt erzielt Draeger durch die Parallelmontage von Szenen aus *Dirty Harry* oder die räumliche Inszenierung seiner Videofilme. Es scheint darum zu gehen, den Bildern des Desasters ihren Ort zuzuweisen. Wir können das Desaster nicht wirklich visualisieren, weil es jeden Rahmen sprengt, wir können es nicht erwarten und nicht kommemorieren, weil es weder vor noch hinter uns liegt, aber man kann es verorten, jedes einzeln. Auch die Puzzles von Katastrophenphotos gehören hierhin: es kann sich nur darum handeln, daß die Dinge – in einem sehr handwerklichen und in einem sehr konzeptuellen Sinne – sich richtig fügen.

Als absolute Singularität erhebt jede Katastrophe einen Anspruch auf Einzigartigkeit. Sie bringt immer die religiöse Spannung ins Vibrieren, die das sakrale Ereignis zwischen der Einzigartigkeit des Opfers und der Universalität der Heilsbotschaft entstehen läßt. Draeger zieht ungerührt zur nächsten Katastrophe weiter. Sie kommt bestimmt, und sie hat bestimmt schon stattgefunden. Wir können sie jedoch auf einer Karte eintragen. Es gibt zu viele Apokalypsen: wir müssen sie lokalisieren.

Referenzen

Jean Baudrillard: *La transparence du Mal,* Paris, Galilée 1990.

Maurice Blanchot: *L'écriture du désastre*, Paris, Gallimard 1980.

Alexandre Kojève, russischer Emigrant, der die Revolution fliehen musste, ist eine der entscheidenden Figuren der französischen Nachkriegsphilosophie. In seinem von 1933–39 durchgeführten Seminar über die hegelsche Religionsphilosophie sass der Gotha der nachfolgenden Intellektuellengeneration, unter andern Sartre, de Beauvoir, Bataille, Lacan und Queneau, auf die er einen grossen Einfluss ausübte. Überzeugt, dass mit der Weltgeschichte auch die Philosophie an ihr Ende gekommen sei, hängte er letztere an den Nagel und wurde ein hoher Beamter im französischen Aussenministerium. Eine Summe seiner Hegelinterpretation erschien 1947 unter dem Titel *Introduction à la lecture de Hegel* bei Gallimard.

it lies neither behind nor in front of us, but we can locate every single catastrophe. Even the puzzles of catastrophe photos belong here: The images – in the conceptual, craftsmanship sense – ordain themselves correctly.

As an absolute singularity, every catastrophe brings forth a demand for uniqueness. It always brings religious tension to vibration, which allows to the sacral event between the uniqueness of the sacrifice and the universal aspect of the message of recovery to come to fruition. Draeger moves, unaffected, to the next catastrophe. It will definitely come, and it has definitely already happened. We can still mark it on a map. There are too many apocalypses, we must localize them.

Translation: Kimberly Bradley, New York

References

Jean Baudrillard: *La transparence du Mal,* Paris, Galilée 1990.

Maurice Blanchot: *L'écriture du désastre*, Paris, Gallimard 1980.

Alexandre Kojeve: Russian emigrant who fled the revolution, is one of the important figures in French postwar philosophy. In a seminar he conducted on Hegelian religious philosophy from 1933–39, he exerted great influence over the following generation of intellectuals: Gotha, Sartre, de Beauvoir, Bataille, Lacan and Queneau. Convinced that philosophy would perish with the end of world history, he gave the discipline up and became a high-level civil servant in the French foreign ministry. A summation of his interpretation of Hegel appeared in 1947 under the title *Introduction à la lecture de Hegel* at Gallimard.

1 **Apocalypse now**
Video VHS 20 min, still from *Gorgo*

2 **Disaster**
unknown

3 **Documenta O (Kassel 1945)**
documenta Archiv, Kassel
Acrylic paint jet on jigsaw puzzle,
7500 pcs, 110 x 260 cm, 1999

4 **Écriture du désastre**
Maurice Blanchot, Edition Gallimard, 1980

5 **The great disasters**
Grosset & Dunlap, 1976

6 **Disaster films**
photo: Christoph Draeger, Tower Records, NY 1999

7, 8, 9 **Apocalypse now**
Video VHS 20 min, stills from *Zabrinskie point*

10 **Apocalypse now**
Video VHS 20 min, still from *Apocalypse now*

11 **Disaster sundays**
photo: Christoph Draeger, NY 1997

12 **Roadsign / Wegweiser**
ca 220 x 50 x 50 cm, metal, aluminium, letters, rendered by Michel Ritter, Kunsthalle Fri-Art, Fribourg (CH), 1996

Voyages apocalyptiques, 1994–99
C-prints, 46 x 58 cm each, edition of 3

Ongoing series of photographies depicting sites where once a disaster happened (see index, p. 92). Dates refer to the day the picture was taken.

Fortlaufende Photoserie von Orten, an denen eine Katastrophe stattfand (s. Index S. 92). Die Daten beziehen sich auf den Tag, an dem die Photographie gemacht wurde.

Galtür, Austria, July 7 1999

Peggy's Cove, Nova Scotia, Canada, Sep 2 1999

World Trade Center, New York City, USA, June 24 1994	Charleston, South Carolina, USA, June 29 1994	Cape Canaveral, Florida, USA, July 1 1994
Malibu, California, USA, Aug 12 1994	San Francisco, California, USA, Aug 17 1994	Mount St. Helens, Washington, USA, Aug 22 1994
Brig, Switzerland, Nov 11 1995	Heysel, Brussels, Belgium, Jan 13 1995	Zeebrugge, Belgium, Feb 2 1995

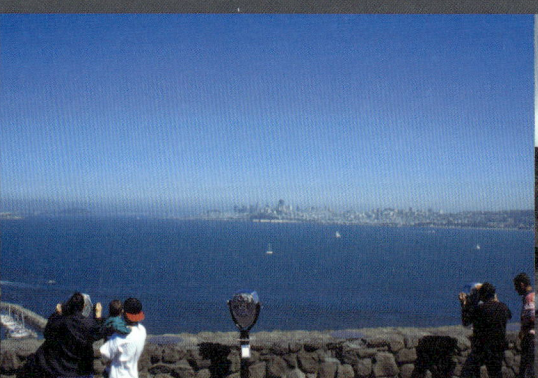

Homestead, Florida, USA, July 7 1994	Alamogordo, New Mexico, USA, July 24 1994	Los Angeles, California, USA, Aug 8 1994
Little Bighorn, Montana, USA, Aug 25 1994	Three Mile Island, Harrisburg, Pennsylvania, USA, Aug 30 1994	Fiumicicoli, Corsica (F), Nov 7 1995
Bijlmermeer, Amsterdam, Netherlands, Feb 9 1995	Schweizerhalle, Basel, Switzerland, March 9 1995	US Airbase Ramstein, Germany, March 28 1995

Kobe, Japan, July 31 1995

Hiroshima, Japan, Aug 4 1995

Nagasaki, Japan, Aug 7 1995

Furiani, Bastia, Corsica (F), May 5 1996

Vaison la Romaine, France, July 8 1997

Los Alfaques, Spain, July 10 1997

Eschede, Germany, Aug 18 1998

Dusseldorf Airport, Germany, Aug 21 1998

Omagh, Northern Ireland (UK), Feb 17 1999

Mt. Unzen, Fugendake, Japan,
Aug 10 1995

Minamata, Japan, Aug 12 1995

Tokyo, Japan, Sep 9 1995

Kwangju, Korea, Aug 31 1997

Seoul, Korea, Sep 5 1997

Pont de l'Alma, Paris, France,
May 9 1998

Derry, Northern Ireland (UK),
June 20 1999

Belfast, Northern Ireland (UK),
June 26 1999

Halifax, Nova Scotia, Canada,
Sep 1 1999

地震 火を消せ！！

Earthquake warning
Poster, Kobe, Japan 1995
ca 30 x 50 cm

Un ga nai – bad luck
Experimental documentary on
disasters in Japan, 1995
Video Hi 8/Beta, 42 min
® usa – united swiss artist, 1995–99
in collaboration with Martin Frei
and Thomas Thümena

Video stills:
Tokyo by night, AUMs' Shoko
Ashahara in the subway, disaster
prevention exercises in Tokyo, fire
station in Ikebukuru, Draeger in
earthquake simulator, reconstruction
of Kobe, Great-to-be-alive-in-95
festival in Kobe, Nagata destroyed
by fire, atomic bomb, victim in Hiroshima, Godzilla, Girl in Nagaski, Sushi.

Film team from left to right:
Ali Durt Morimoto, Martin Frei,
Christoph Draeger in Nagasaki,
August 7 1995

Mount Unzen-Fugendake, August 10
4 years after eruption

Sakurashima 1914
Acrylic paint jet on rice paper,
80 x 160 cm, photographer unknown
® usa – united swiss artist, 1998
In collaboration with Martin Frei

Sakurashima 1995 / toy volcano
Acrylic paint jet on rice paper,
80 x 120 cm, photo: Christoph Draeger
® usa – united swiss artist, 1998
In collaboration with Martin Frei

Un ga nai - bad luck, video still
House buried in the mud after
the eruption of Mount Unzen (1991)

Tokyo, September 1 1995
Photo series of the annual disaster prevention exercises, commemorating the Kanto earthquake in Tokyo, 1923

Un ga nai – bad luck
Outtakes from the project
® usa – united swiss artist, 1995
Photos: Martin Frei / Christoph Draeger

It's the end of the world as we love it
Installation view
Shed im Eisenwerk, Frauenfeld (CH), 1996
A project of Christoph Draeger and Martin Frei, co-curated by Harm Lux feat. Pascale Wiedemann, Roman Signer, Bessie Nager, Urs Lehmann, Ali Durt Morimoto, Claire Durlin, Ganzer Platz, Gianni Motti

Un ga nai – bad luck, video still

73

18 250 days after
Hiroshima, August 6 1995, 8:15 a.m.
Nagasaki, August 9 1995, 11:02 a.m.

(The photos were taken precisely
50 years after the atomic bombs were
dropped on the two cities)

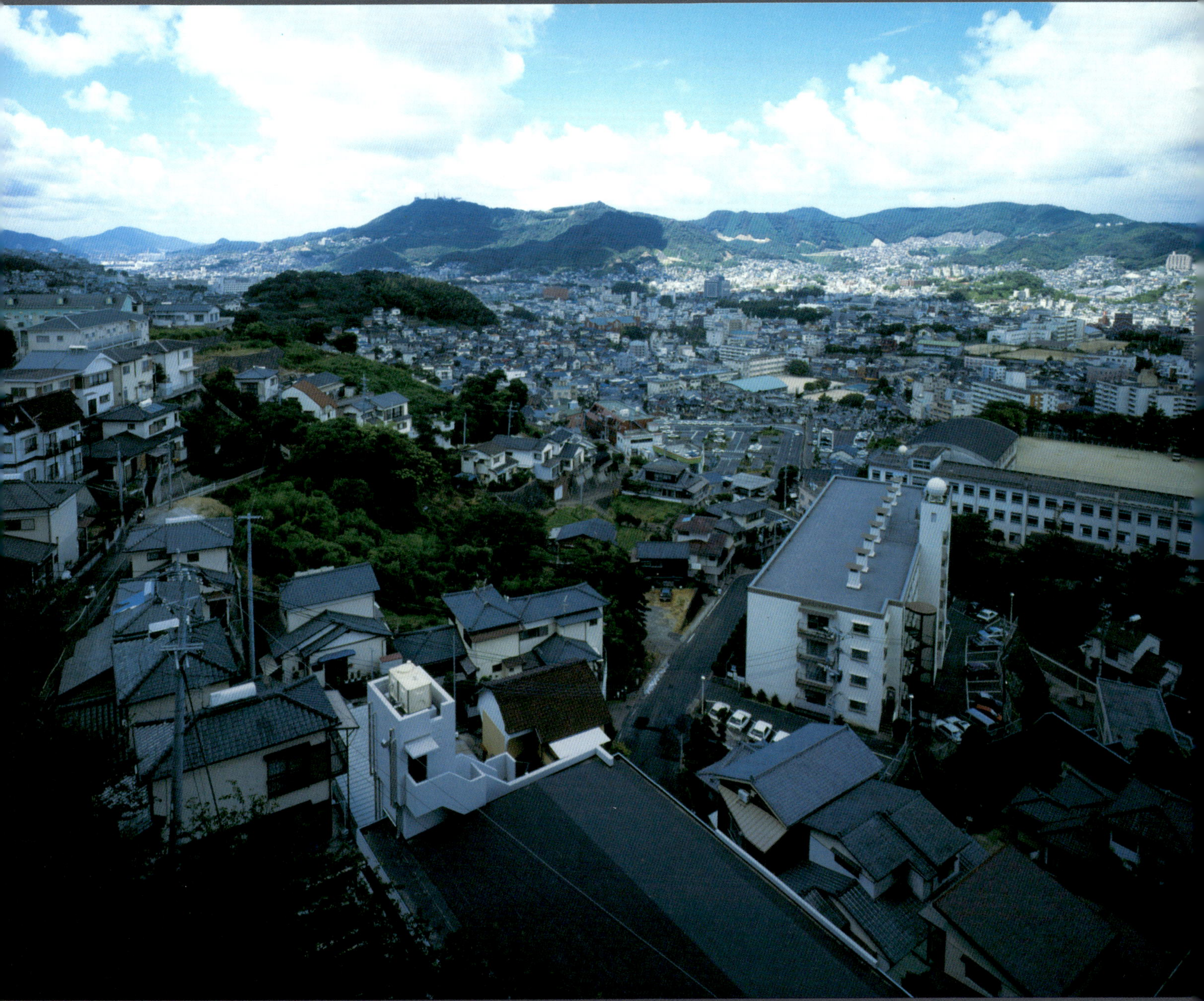

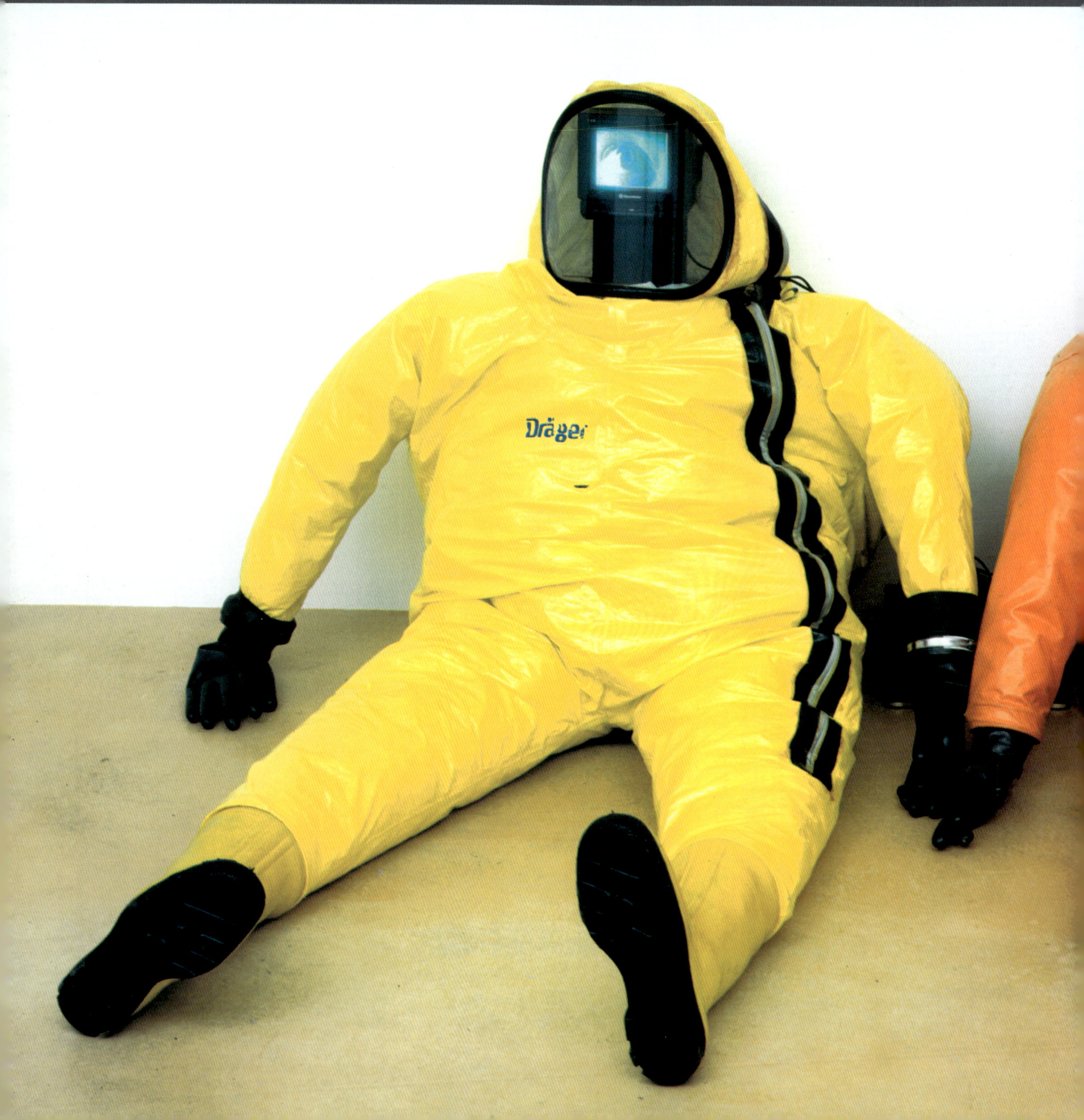
Dräger

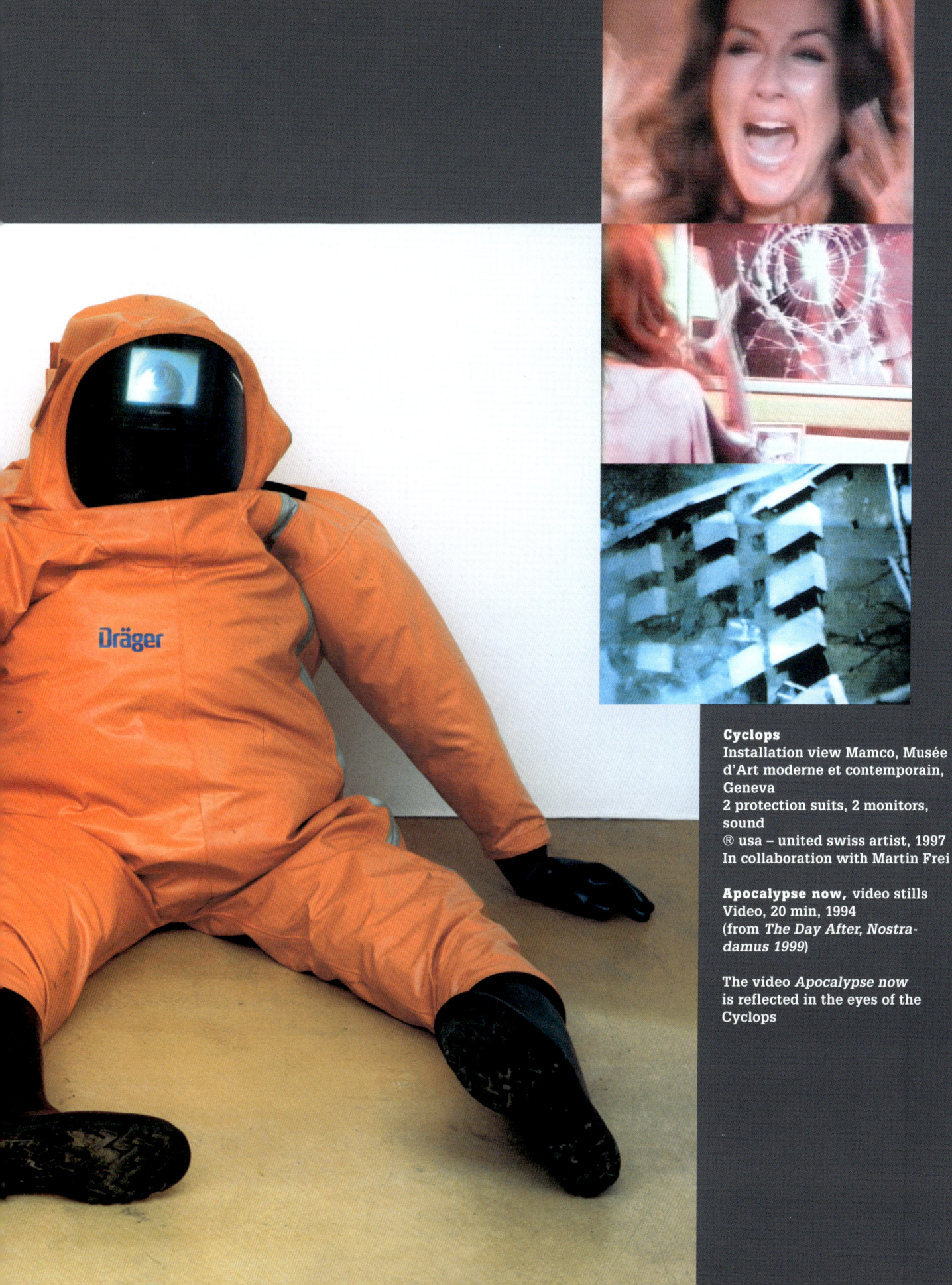

Cyclops
Installation view Mamco, Musée d'Art moderne et contemporain, Geneva
2 protection suits, 2 monitors, sound
® usa – united swiss artist, 1997
In collaboration with Martin Frei

Apocalypse now, video stills
Video, 20 min, 1994
(from *The Day After, Nostradamus 1999*)

The video *Apocalypse now* is reflected in the eyes of the Cyclops

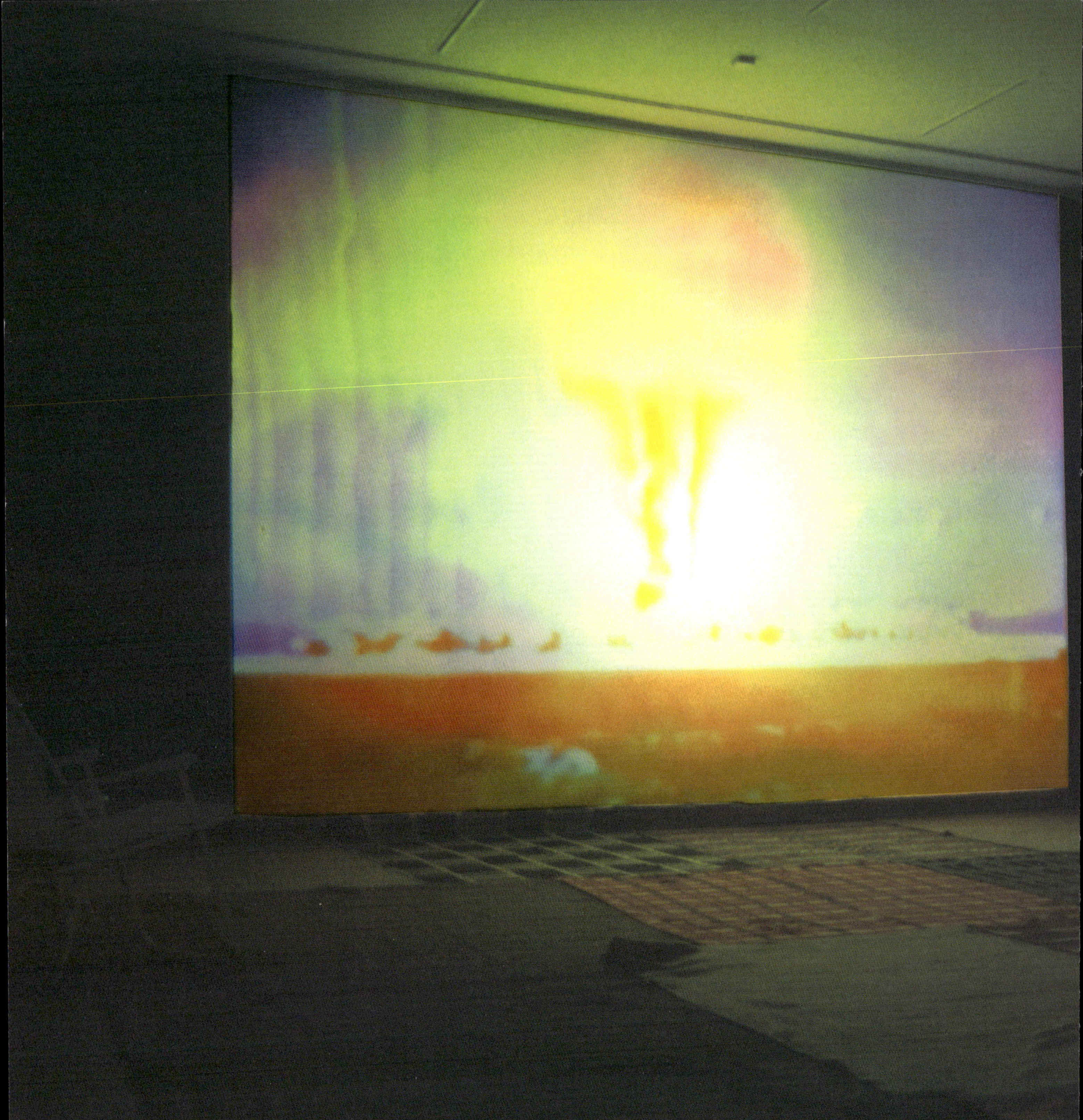

Yellow & Red
Installation view
ICA-D, Institute for Contemporary Art,
Dunauyvaros (Hungary)
® usa – united swiss artist, 1999
In collaboration with Martin Frei and
Thomas Thümena

Yellow & Red, video stills
Video, 16mm / Hi-8, 10 min
® usa – united swiss artist, 1999

Catastrophe #2
Acrylic paint jet on pvc, 300 x 400 cm
Model: 120m²
Trash, plaster, wood, pigments, etc
Brussels, 1994–96

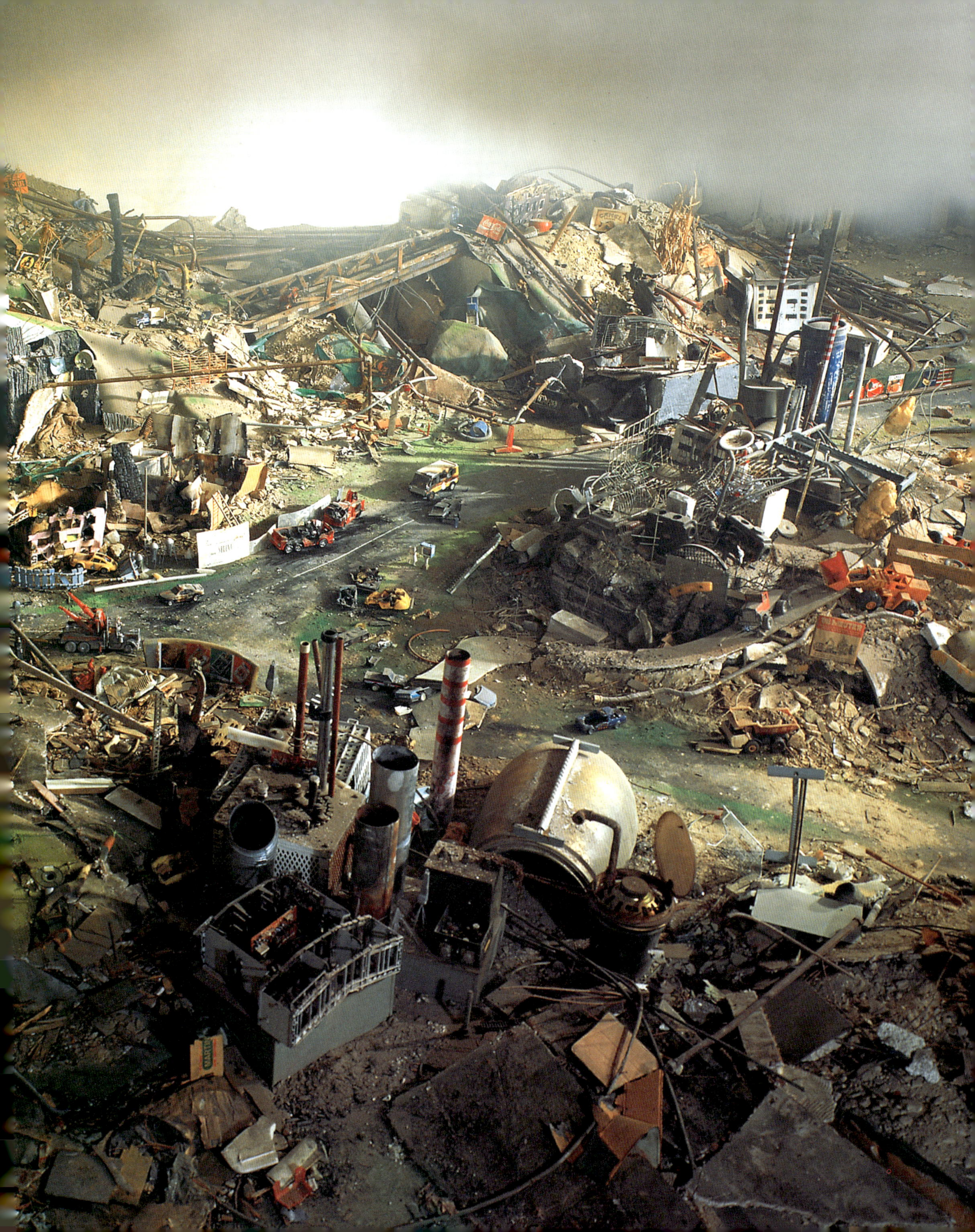

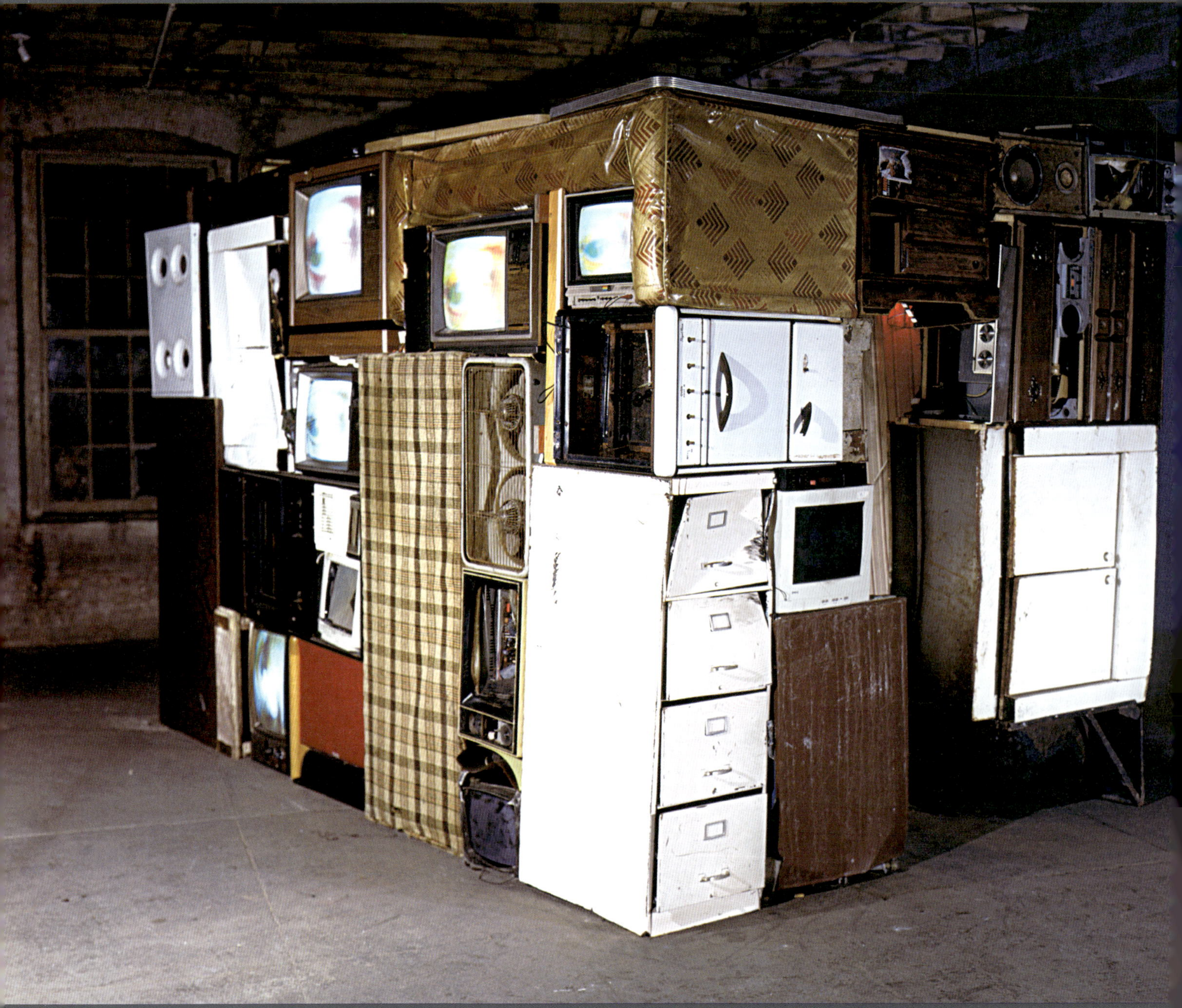

System 3
Installation view Roebling Hall, New York
11 TVs, furniture, trash
In collaboration with Reynold Reynolds

Videos:
(Front wall)
The history of the future
Reynold Reynolds
Found footage of ca 60 science fiction movies, video VHS, 15 min, 1996

(Back wall)
Apocalypse now
® usa – united swiss artist
Found footage of ca 50 disaster movies, video VHS, 1994

(Interior)
The three days of darkness
Found footage of end of the world prophecies, video VHS 90 min, 1996

Oel, (oil), video still
Video Beta SP, 13 min, 1998

86

Oelteppich (oilslick)
Installation view Galerie Urs Meile, Lucerne
Video projection, sound, water, oil
1998

Oel, (oil), video stills
Found footage
Video VHS / Beta SP, 13 min, 1998
(from *Waterworld, The Prize, Speed 2*)

Oilslick / Major oil spills
Installation views
Galerie Damasquine, Brussels
Video projection, sound, water, oil, gangway
25 paintings, oil on canvas, rendered by Arnold Helbling
1999

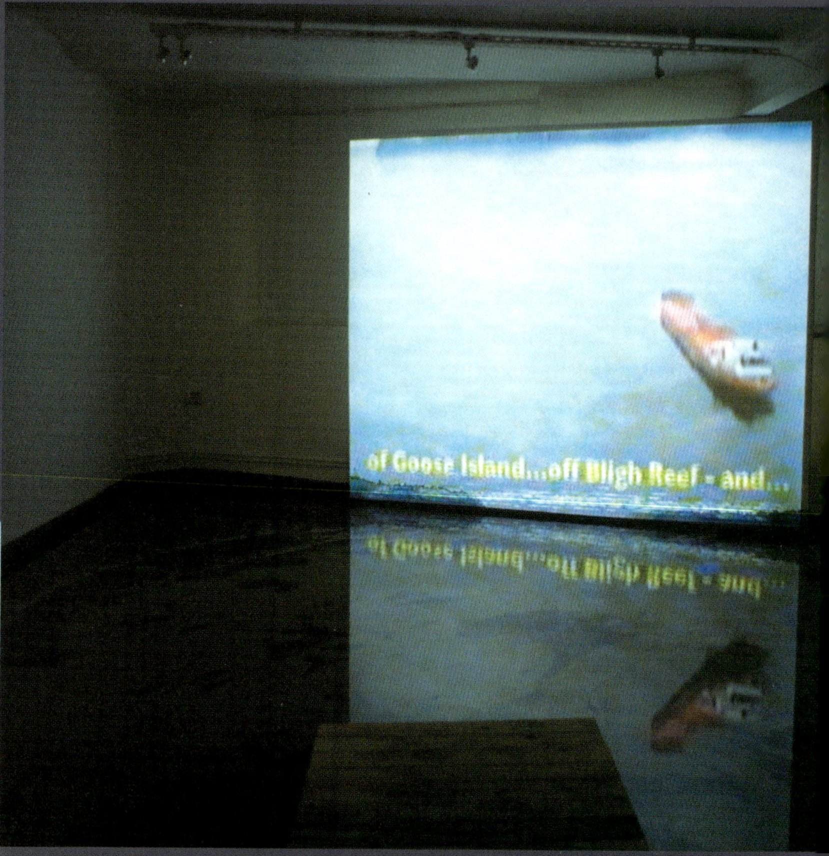
of Goose Island...off Bligh Reef - and...

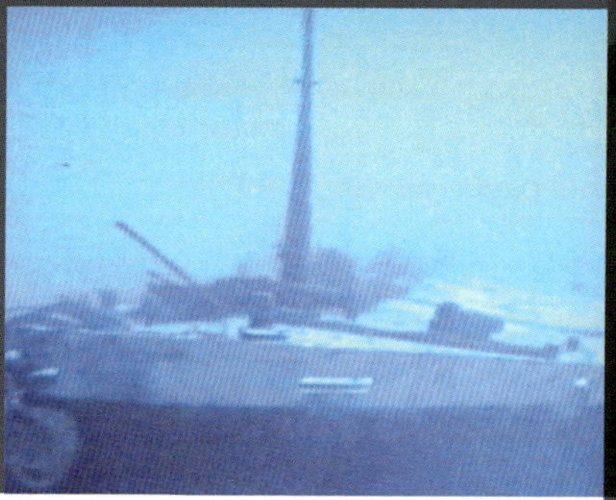

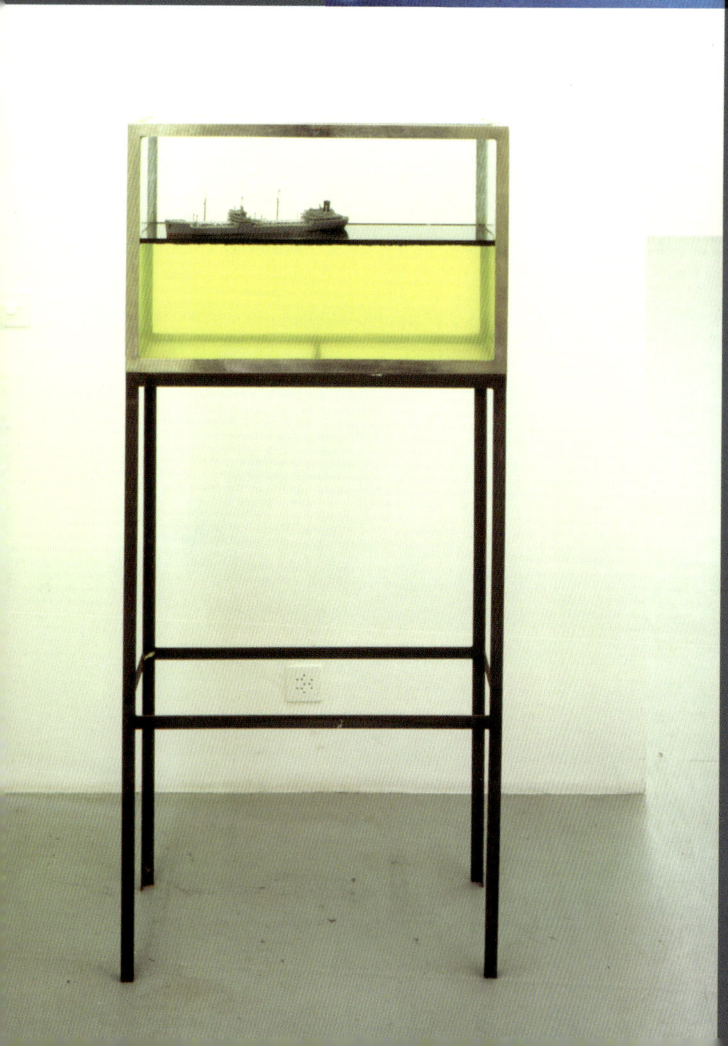

Oeltank (oil tank)
Aquarium, oil tanker model, water, used oil, 1998

Oelteppich (oilslick)
Installation view Galerie Damasquine, Brussels
Video projection, sound, water, oil, gangway
1999

Major oil spills
Installation view Galerie Urs Meile, Lucerne
25 paintings, oil on canvas, various formats
(ca 30 x 50 cm each),
rendered by Arnold Helbling
1998

Oel (oil)
Video stills
Video VHS (found footage) / Beta SP, 13 min, 1998
(from *The Spy Who Loved Me*, *The Prize*)

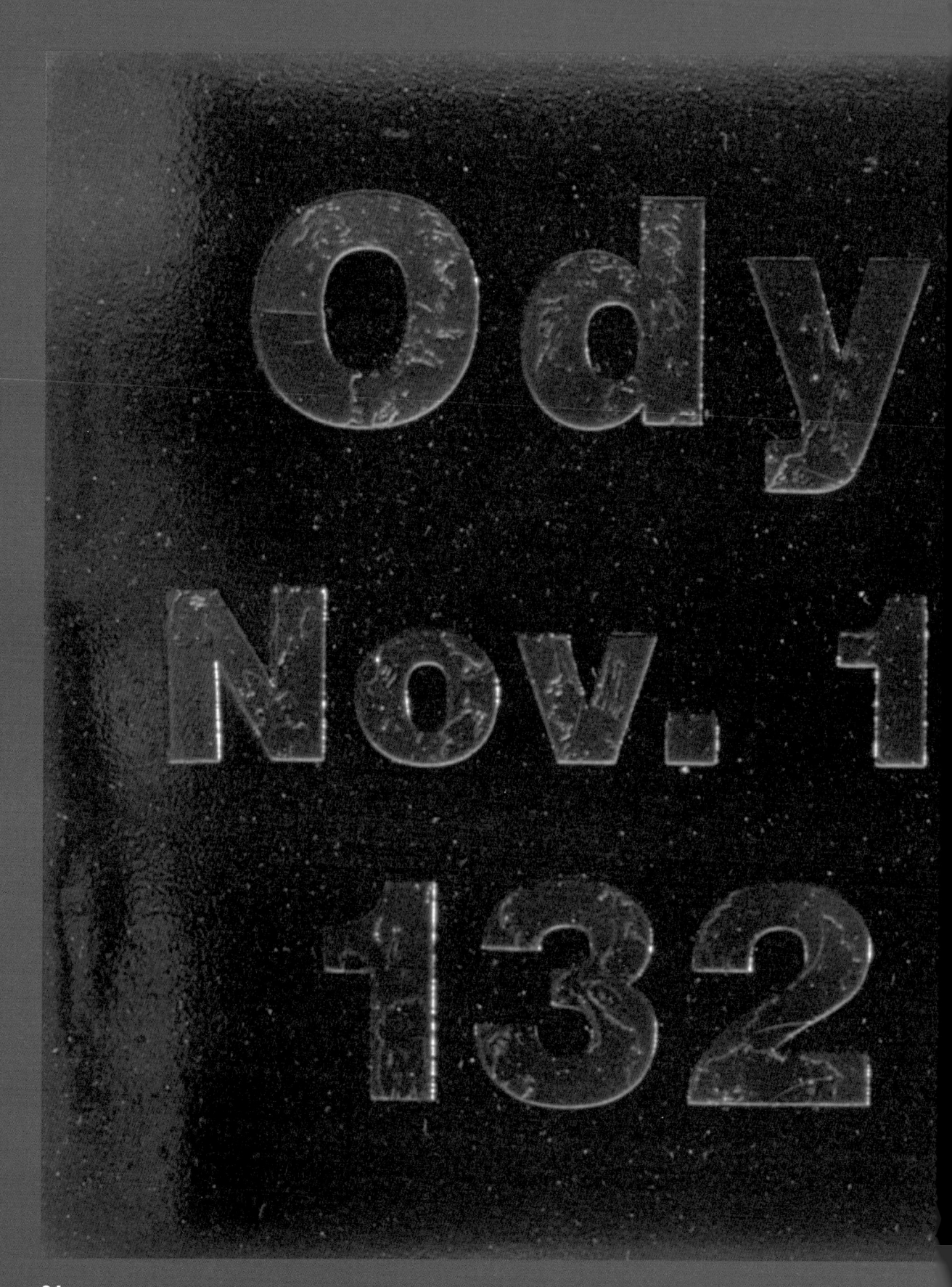

Odyssey
From the series *Major oil spills*
Oil on canvas, 26 x 42 cm, rendered by Arnold Helbling
1998

ssey

1988

000

Index of *Voyages apocalyptiques* 1994–99

World Trade Center, New York City, USA, June 24 1994
5†, Terrorist bombing / Bombenattentat, Feb 26 1993

Charleston, South Carolina, USA, June 29 1994
20†, Hurricane Hugo / Wirbelsturm, Sep 2 1989

Cape Canaveral, Florida, USA, July 1 1994
7†, Challenger disaster / Space Shuttle Challenger explodiert, Jan 28 1987

Homestead, Florida, USA, July 7 1994
22†, Hurricane Andrew / Wirbelsturm, Aug 24 1992

Alamogordo, New Mexico, USA, July 24 1994
"Trinity", First atomic bomb test / 1. Atombombentest, July 16 1945

Los Angeles, California, USA, Aug 8 1994
58†, Rodney King riots / Rodney King-Unruhen, April 29 1992
Last earthquake / Letztes Erdbeben, Jan 19 1994

Malibu, California, USA, Aug 12 1994
3†, Brush fires / Buschfeuer im Villenquartier, Oct 26 1992

San Francisco, California, USA, Aug 17 1994
700† / 66†, Earthquakes / Erdbeben, Apr 18 1908 / Jan 19 1989

Mount St. Helens, Washington, USA, Aug 22 1994
57†, Volcanic eruption / Vulkanausbruch, May 18 1980

Little Bighorn, Montana, USA, Aug 25 1994
220†, Indian battle / Indianerschlacht, June 25 1876

Three Mile Island, Harrisburg, Pennsylvania, USA, Aug 30 1994
Nuclear meltdown / Reaktorunglück, March 28 1979

Fiumicicoli, Corsica (F), Nov 7 1995
2†, Flood / Überschwemmung, Nov 7 1993

Brig, Switzerland, Nov 11 1995
2†, Flood / Überschwemmung, 1995

Heysel, Brussels, Belgium, Jan 13 1995
41†, Hooligan riot / Aufruhr im Fussballstadium, May 29 1985

Zeebrugge, Belgium, Feb 6 1995
41†, Ferry capsized / Fährenunglück, March 6 1987

Bijlmermeer, Amsterdam, Netherlands, Feb 9 1995
47†, El-Al plane crash into building / El Al-Absturz auf Wohnblock, Oct 4 1992

Schweizerhalle, Basel, Switzerland, March 9 1995
Fire in chemical plant / Grossfeuer in Chemiewerk, Nov 1 1986

US Airbase Ramstein, Germany, March 28 1995
61†, Midair collision during airshow / Crash bei Flugschau, Aug 22 1988

Kobe, Japan, July 31 1995
5000†, Hanshin-earthquake / Erdbeben, Jan 17 1995

Hiroshima, Japan, Aug 4 1995
200 000†, First atomic bomb dropped on a city / Erster Atombombenabwurf, Aug 6 1945

Nagasaki, Japan, Aug 7 1995
120 000†, Last atomic bomb dropped on a city / Letzter Atombombenabwurf, Aug 9 1945

Mt. Unzen, Fugendake, Japan, Aug 10 1995
45†, Volcanic eruption / Vulkanausbruch, June 3 1991

Minamata, Japan, Aug 12 1995
1000†, Mercury poisoning of the seashore from the 1950's / Quecksilbervergiftung seit 1950

Tokyo, Japan, Sep 9 1995
170 000†, Japan's worst earthquake / Japans schwerstes Erdbeben, Sep 1 1923
11†, Terrorist assault on subway system (Sarin gas) / Giftgasanschlag in der Metro, Mar 20 1995

Furiani, Bastia, Corsica (F), May 5 1996
17†, Tribune crashes during soccer match / Tribüneneinsturz, May 5 1992

Vaison la Romaine, France, July 8 1997
34†, Flash flood in campground / Überschwemmung in Camping, Sep 22 1992

Los Alfaques, Spain, July 10 1997
180†, Gasoline truck explosion on campground / Tankwagenexplosion in Camping, June 11 1978

Kwangju, Korea, Aug 31 1997
Hundreds † / Hunderte †, Military massacre during student riots / Massaker während Studentenunruhen, May 9 1980

Seoul, Korea, Sep 5 1997
501†, Departement store collapses / Warenhauseinsturz, June 29 1995

Pont de l'Alma, Paris, France, May 9 1998
3†, Car accident Diana and Dodi / Autounfall Diana und Dodi, Aug 31 1997

Eschede, Germany, Aug 18 1998
102†, ICE 884 derails / ICE Entgleisung, June 3 1998

Dusseldorf Airport, Germany, Aug 21 1998
17†, Fire in elevator / Brand im Aufzug, Nov 4 1996

Omagh, Northern Ireland (UK), Feb 17 1999
29†, IRA terrorist bombing / IRA-Bombe, Aug 15 1998

Derry, Northern Ireland (UK), June 20 1999
14†, Bloody Sunday: massacre by British paratroopers / Blutiger Sonntag: Massaker durch britische Luftlandetruppen, Jan 30 1972

Belfast, Northern Ireland (UK), June 26 1999
Hundreds † / Hunderte †, Civil war / Bürgerkrieg, since / seit 1968

Galtür, Austria, July 7 1999
43†, Avalanche hits village / Tallawine, Feb 23 1999

Lakehurst, New Jersey, Aug 13 1999
34†, Airship Hindenburg crash lands / Zeppelin-Absturz, May 6 1937

Halifax, Nova Scotia, Canada, Sep 1 1999
11 000†, Greatest man-made explosion (TNT) before atomic bomb / Grösste vom Menschen verursachte Explosion (TNT) vor der Atombombe, 1917

Peggy's Cove, Nova Scotia, Canada, Sep 2 1999
229†, Flight SR 111 crashes into sea after cockpit fire / Swissair 111 stürzt nach Cockpit-Brand ins Meer, Sep 2 1998

to be continued / Fortsetzung folgt

Christoph Draeger

265 Mc Kibbin St, 3rd floor
11206 Brooklyn NY USA
Tel/Fax: 001 718 628 11 29
E-mail: draegerusa@thing.net

4. 8. 1965	Born in Zurich
1985	Matura in Schiers
1986–90	School of Visual Arts Lucerne, Diploma
1990–91	École Nationale Supérieure des Arts Visuels de la Cambre, Brussels
1990–95	Lives and works in Brussels
1996/97	P.S.1, Institute for Contemporary Art, New York
since 1996	Lives and works in New York

Christoph Draeger visiting the site of impact of Swissair flight 111, Peggy's Cove, Nova Scotia, Canada, Sep 2 1999

Solo Exhibitions

1999 *Apocalypso Place*
Liebman Magnan Gallery, New York
(in collaboration with Reynold Reynolds)

Crash
Förderkoje, Galerie Urs Meile, Art Cologne

Lakehurst, New Jersey
Grenz-Raum, Zeppelin Museum
Friedrichshafen (D)*

Voyages apocalyptiques
Stalke Gallery, Copenhagen

Action//Time//Vision (Alternative TV)
Orchard Gallery, Derry, (Northern Ireland)*

Out of the Blue – Into the Black
Damasquine Gallery, Brussels

1998 *New York Serneus retour*
Kulturhaus Rosengarten, Grüsch (CH)*

Make Believe
Stalke Gallery, Copenhagen
(with Per Traasdaal, Susann Walder)*

Puzzled
Statements, Galerie Urs Meile,
Art 29, Basel*

OEL
Galerie Urs Meile, Lucerne

NB
Kunsthalle, St.Gall (with Biefer/Zgraggen)*

Hotelbrand
Hotel, Zurich

1997 *Nature abhoars a naked singularity*
Clocktower Gallery, New York
(with Nina Bruderman, Patrick Jolley)

1996 *How far you are*
Passage Placette, Belluard Fribourg (CH)
(organised by Kunsthalle FriArt)

1995 *The apartment*
Filiale Basel* (with Gianni Motti,
Alexandre Biancini)

Think Apocalypse,
Galerie Observatoire, Brussels
(with Andy Best, Olivier Nolin)

1993 *Critical Distance,*
ADO Gallery, Antwerp (with OCI)*

Schleutelwerken
Galerie Fons Welters, Amsterdam
(with OCI)*

1991 *Solo*
Etablissements d'en Face, Brussels*

* catalogue

Group Exhibitions (selection)

1999 *Amnesic Cinemas*
Galerie du Bellay, Rouen (F)

Out of Order
Roebling Hall, New York

Autour de R2/12
Attitudes, Geneva (CH)

Cinéma, Cinéma
Stedelijk Van Abbe Museum, Eindhoven (NL)

Playtime
Magasin, Grenoble (F)

1998 *Dystopia/Babel*
Roebling Hall, New York

*Mütter, ihr habt's ja so gewollt /
Mothers, you got what you wanted*
ACC Galerie, Weimar (D)

Reservate der Sehnsucht / Zones of Desire
Unionbrauerei, Dortmund*

diana.98
Xtra Limmathaus, Zurich
(organised by Migros Museum, Zurich)

Videoforum
Art '29, Basel

*De très courts espaces de temps /
Very short spaces of time*
Biennale de l'image, CNP,
École des Beaux-Arts, Paris*

1997 *P.S.1 International Studio Show*
Clocktower Gallery, New York*

Kiosk
Downtown Art Festival, New York

Disaster and Recovery
The Swiss Institute, New York

Young Art
Mamco, musée d'Art contemporain, Geneva

VideoVisions 2
El Haganar, Cairo

1996 *Le meridien de Verviers*
Musée des Beaux-Arts, Verviers (B)*

Young Art
Kunsthalle, Berne*

Picture this
Dennis Anderson Gallery, Antwerp

*Begrenzte Grenzenlosigkeit /
Bounds of Boundlessness*
NGBK, Berlin*

1995 *Étalage*
Comptoir, Brussels*

1994 *Prospectus*
Laeken-Brussels (B)*

Prix du club 51
Musée d'Art moderne, Liège (B)

Photographies
Galerie Rodolphe Janssen, Brussels

Jeune peinture Belge
Palais des Beaux-Arts, Brussels*

Preisträger / Award winners
Musée d'Art et Histoire, Neuchâtel (CH)*

Variations sur le charme discret de la bourgoisie
Observatoire Gallery, London

1993 *Members Only*
Charles Poy Gallery, Barcelona*

1992 *In der Kälte / In the cold*
Kunsthalle Lucerne*

Video screenings (selection)

1999 CIC, Centre pour l'image Contemporain
St. Gervais, Geneva

Tramvideo
Lyon (F)

Le Club du Capitain Pip
Centre d'art contemporain
Espace Jules Verne, Bretigny sur Orge (F)

1998 *Armageddon now*
Kino Loge, Winterthur (CH)*

The Videoroom Festival
Ocularis, New York

Lost & Found
De Waag, Amsterdam

1997 *Videos for an unknown channel*
Moving Art Studio, Brussels

*   catalogue

Grants

1999 Grant of the Government of Kanton Graubünden (CH)
1996 Atelier der Eidgenossenschaft / P.S.1 – International Studio Program Grant, New York
1995 Kiefer-Hablitzel Award (CH)
1994 Eidgenössischer Preis für freie Kunst / Swiss National Art Award
1994 Kiefer-Hablitzel Award (CH)
       Club 51 Award, Liège (B)
1990 Award of the Landis & Gyr Foundation (CH)
1991–99 Numerous grants of the Art Council of Kanton Graubünden (CH)

Public Collections

Musée d'Art et histoire Neuchatel

Kunst Heute Foundation, Bern

Communauté francaise, Brussels

Bündner Kunstmuseum, Chur

CIC – centre pour l'image contemporain, St. Gervais, Geneva

Bibliography (selection)

Luk Lambrecht, *Solo – Etablissement d'en face, Brussels,* DeMorgen, 9/1991

Martin Frei, *catastrophy,* catalogue *OCI and Christoph Draeger,* ADO Gallery Antwerp, 1993

Jean-Paul Jaquet, *Voyages apocalyptiques,* Etant donné, Brussels, 5/1993

Lino Polegato, *construire la déstruction,* Flux News, Liège, 9/1993

Margaret Jardas, *4 junge Schweizer – Filiale Basel,* Basler Zeitung, 3/95

Thomas Seelig, *Christoph Draeger,* Pakt, Zeitschrift für zeitgenösische Kunst, 1/96

Paolo Bianci, *Apokalyptische Reisen,* Kunstforum 137, 6/97

Christoph Doswald, Interview, Facts 12/97

Pierre-André Lienhard, *Hat der Weltuntergang schon stattgefunden?,* catalogue NB, 12/98

Edith Arnold, *Immer modischer,* Interview, Neue Luzerner Zeitung, 3/98

Maria Vogel, *Aestetisch untadelig vorgeführte Katastrophen,* Neue Luzerner Zeitung, 4/98

Cecile Bourne, *Feel Lucky, Punk??!,* catalogue Biennale de l'image Paris, 1998

Pascal Beausse, *Zoe Beloff / Christoph Draeger After-images,* Art Press 235, 5/98

Gerhard Mack, *Heulende Sirenen im Telekolleg,* NB – Kunsthalle St. Gallen, Tagblatt 2/98

Samuel Herzog, *Schaschlik aus Half Brain und Dirty Harry,* videoforum ART 29, Basler Zeitung 6/98

Christoph Doswald, *Make Believe: Artistic Self-Assertion in the Age of Autopoetic Simulation,* catalogue *Make Believe,* Stalke Gallery, Copenhagen, 1998

Gerhard Mack, *Seine Kunst ist eine einzige Katastrophe,* CASH, 8/98

Gisela Kuoni, *Von Katastrophen im Prättigau,* Buendner Zeitung 10/98

Peter Masüger, *New York Serneus retour,* Bündner Tagblatt 11/98

Christoph Doswald, *Apocalypse, Now?,* Katalog *Cinéma, Cinéma,* Van Abbe Museum Eindhoven 2/99

Bernhard Marcelis, *Christoph Draeger / Galerie Damasquine,* Artpress 246, Mai 99

Beatrice Ruf, *Christoph Draeger,* in *Art at Ringier 1995–1998,* catalogue, 1999

Action//Time//Vision, The Guardian, 7/99

Padraig Timoney, *Christoph Draeger / The Orchard Gallery,* Art Monthly, 9/99

Beat Stutzer, *Die Aura des Todes als Bildthema,* Die Südostschweiz, 9/99

® usa – united swiss artist: Christoph Draeger and Martin Frei

Solo Exhibitions

1999 *Yellow and Red*
Institute for Contemporary Art,
Dunauyvarnos, (Hungary)

1998 *Heidji*
Galerie Luciano Fascati, Chur (CH)

Kommerzbau
Galerie Berhard Schindler, Berne (CH)

1997 *Life on mars*
Kunst 97 Zürich
(Galerie Bernhard Schindler, Berne)

1996 *It's the end of the world as we love it*
Shed im Eisenwerk, Frauenfeld (CH)

1995 *Die grosse Überfahrt / The great crossing* +
Erfrischungsraum, Lucerne

Un ga nai – bad luck
Documentary film project, Japan

1994 *M.U.S.E.U.M.*+
Kunstmuseum Lucerne* (CH)

© USA in Amerika
Pinkus Gallery, New York

1990 *Schlaraffenland*++
HeiQel, Zurich

Am Ende die Kunst+++
Trip Galerie, Lucerne

1988 *Nature morte*+++
Schule für Gestaltung, Lucerne

* catalogue
+ with Rebecca Schmid, Urs Lehmann
++ with Mona Jenni, Urs Lehmann
+++ with Urs Lehmann

Group Exhibitions

1999 *Videos aus der Sammlung / Video Collection*
Un ga nai – bad luck,
Kunsthaus, Zurich

Dog days are over
Centre Culturel Suisse, Paris

Videolounge
Freie Sicht aufs Mittelmeer,
Kunsthaus Zurich*

1997 2nd Biennal, *Speed*
(curated by Harald Szeemann)
Kwangju, Corea*

1995 *Sicherheit und Zusammenarbeit*
Museum für Gestaltung, Zurich

Vision – Illusion – Realität
Kunsthaus, Zurich

Jedes Haus ein Kunsthaus
Museum für Gestaltung, Zurich

* catalogue

Video Screenings (selection)

1999 *Un ga nai – bad luck*
Documentary Film Festival, Duisburg (D)

Un ga nai – bad luck
VIPER, International Video und Film
Festival, Lucerne

Un ga nai – bad luck
Chicago Underground Film Festival

Apocalypse now
CIC, centre pour l'image contemporain,
St. Gervais, Geneva

Un ga nai – bad luck
New York Underground Film Festival

1997 *Un ga nai, Apocalypse now, Life on mars*
St. Gervais Videofestival, Attitudes,
Geneva

Grants

1994/99 Werkbeiträge,
Swiss National Art Council, Berne

1995/98 Grants of the Art Council of Kanton
Graubünden (CH)

Public Collections

Kunsthaus, Zurich

Kunstmuseum, Lucerne

CIC – centre pour l'image contemporain,
St. Gervais, Geneva

Stadt Chur (CH)

Bibliography

Maria Vogel, *Die Kunst am Ende?*,
LNN Lucerne 4/1990

Hans-Peter Wittwer, catalogue *M.U.S.E.U.M.*,
Kunstmuseum Lucerne, 1994

Maria Vogel, *Die grosse Überfahrt*,
LNN Lucerne 10/1995

Kommerzbau, Berner Zeitung, 4/98

Gisela Kuoni, *Christoph Draeger / Martin Frei bei Luciano Fascati*, Kunstbulletin 9/98

Gisela Kuoni, *Leben auf dem Vulkan*,
Bündner Zeitung, 8.9.98

Peter Masüger, *Katastrophen und Klischees*,
Bündner Tagblatt 30.9.98

Werkgespräch mit Dorothea Strauss, catalogue
Galerie Luciano Fascati, Chur (CH) 9/98

Gisela Kuoni, *Die Katastrophe als Kunstwerk*,
Bündner Zeitung, 18.9.98

Impressum

Publisher/Herausgeber
Zeppelin Museum Friedrichshafen, Germany
The Orchard Gallery, Derry, Northern Ireland
Galerie Urs Meile, Lucerne and Christoph Draeger

Co-published by PASSIM, inc., Publisher of Trans>arts.cultures.media, New York

Design/Gestaltung
vista point, Basel

Copy Editing/Redaktion
Kim Bradley, Christian Viveros-Fauné

Printing/Druck
Druck und Verlag Robert Gessler GmbH&Co. KG, Friedrichshafen

Copyright
©1999, the publishers, Christoph Draeger, the photographers and the authors
bei den Herausgebern, Christoph Draeger, den Photographen und den Autoren

ISBN 1-888209-06-2 (for the U.S.)
ISBN 3-86136-046-2 (for Europe)
Library of Congress Catalog Card Number: 99-75809
Printed in Germany

This book is dedicated to Paula

Thanks/Dank
I would like to thank the following persons for their help:
Herzlichen Dank für ihre Unterstützung:

Heidrun Holzfeind (New York), Sibylle Ryser (Basel), Urs Meile (Lucerne), Johannes Schütt and Monika Walter (Diessenhofen), Jules Spinatsch (Zurich), Arnold Helbling (New York), Reynold Reynolds (New York), Dirk Blübaum and Wolfgang Meighörner (Friedrichshafen), Martin Frei (New York), Claire Durlin (Paris), Norbert Leimeister (Marktheidenfeld), Kim Bradley (New York), Sandra Antelo-Suarez (New York), Christian Viveros-Fauné and Joel Beck (New York), Kathy Magnan and Penny Liebmann (New York), Reto Rossi (Höri), Brendan McMenamin and Seamus Boyle (Derry), Josef and Abraham Sayoun (Earthquake of San Francisco), Oliver Kress (Dräger CH), Nina Brudermann, Gary Breslin (PanOptics, New York), Georg Jenni and Rico Padrun (Grüsch), Susi and Peter, Matthias and Urs Draeger (Serneus)

This catalogue was made possible due to the generous support by:
Dieser Katalog wurde ermöglicht dank der großzügigen Unterstützung durch:

Derry City Council
Zeppelin Museum Friedrichshafen
Stiftung zum Rosengarten, Grüsch
Pro Helvetia
Kanton Graubünden
Kanton Basel-Stadt
Stiftung Erna und Curt Burgauer
Anni Castie Stiftung

Thanks to all those who couldn't be mentioned before printing.
Allen, die hier vor der Drucklegung nicht mehr erwähnt werden konnten, sei herzlich gedankt.

Photo credits/copyrights (in order of appearance)
Ringier Dokumentation Bild, (front cover)
Christoph Draeger (pp 2, 7, 40, 43, 52/53, 54/55, 62–67, 69, 71, 72)
Rüdiger Schall, Friedrichshafen, (pp 4/5, p 9)
Hans Sonneveld (pp 6, 24/25, 80/81)
Universal Pictures (p 9)
CNN Archives Atlanta/Christoph Draeger (pp 14/15)
Jules Spinatsch (pp 16, 41, 46/47, 48/49, 50/51)
Photo DPA, courtesy of Belga, Brussels (p 16)
Ingo Wagner, EPA Photo DPA, courtesy of Belga, Brussels (p 17)
Kristien Daen, courtesy ADO Gallery, Antwerp (pp 18/19)
Tony Ranze, EPA Photo DPA, courtesy of Belga, Brussels (p 20)
EPA Photo AFP, courtesy of Belga, Brussels (p 21)
Greg Latza, EPA/AFP Photo, courtesy of Belga, Brussels (p 22)
J.J. Scherschel, National Geographic, (p 23, above)
Yonhap, EPA Photo AFP, courtesy of Belga, Brussels (p 23, below)
Reynold Reynolds, courtesy Liebman Magnan, New York (pp 17, 20, 22, repros)
Brendan McMenamin, courtesy The Orchard Gallery, Derry (pp 34/35, 38)
Heidrun Holzfeind (pp 36/37, 38/39, 44/45, 78/79, 84/85, 92)
Peter Cox, courtesy Van Abbe Museum, Eindhoven (p 42)
Patrick Jolley, Swiss Institute (pp 50/51)
Martin Frei (pp 66/67 (Fugendake, Seoul), 69, 72)
Photographer unknown, Japan 1914 (p 68)
Urs Lehmann (p 73)
Sayuri Yoshioka (p 74)
Hideki Kani (p 75)
Ilmari Kalkinnen, courtesy MAMCO, musee d'Art Contemporain, Geneva (pp 76/77)
Thomas Thuemena (p 79, video stills)
Arnold Helbling (pp 82/83, 90/91)
Jean-Pierre Grüter, courtesy Galerie Urs Meile, Lucerne (pp 17, 23, 86, 87/89)
Dominique Bourrée, courtesy Damasquine Gallery, Brussels (pp 87, 88)

ZEPPELIN MUSEUM FRIEDRICHSHAFEN
TECHNIK UND KUNST

The Orchard Gallery, Derry City Council, Orchard Street, Derry BT 48 6E9
The Orchard Gallery is a Derry City Council facility supported in part by the Arts Council of Northern Ireland and with support for its Educational Programme and Community Programme from private trusts and sponsors.

ARTS COUNCIL of Northern Ireland

Kulturförderungskommission **Kanton Graubünden**

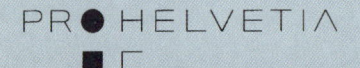

PRO HELVETIA

Challenger
Acrylic paint jet on jigsaw puzzle, 8000 pcs, 136 x 192 cm, 1999
(front cover)

Wutpaki National Monument (detail)
Bubble jet print on canvas, 90 x 120 cm, 1994
(back cover)

Carte apocalyptique du monde 10/99
Dimensions variable, constantly upgraded
Map design is based upon an idea of Richard Buckminster Fuller, rendered by Jens-Ingo Brodesser, since 1994
(cover inside)